# A HISTORY OF STAFFORDSHIRE

*West front of Lichfield Cathedral*

THE DARWEN COUNTY HISTORY SERIES

# A History of Staffordshire

## M. W. GREENSLADE and D. G. STUART

*Drawings by* Carolyn Drouin

*Cartography by* Jayne Southfield and M. J. Naldrett

PHILLIMORE

*First published 1965*
Second edition 1984

Published by
PHILLIMORE & CO. LTD.,
Shopwyke Hall, Chichester, Sussex

© M. W. Greenslade and D. G. Stuart, 1965, 1984

ISBN 0 85033 476 4

Printed and bound in Great Britain by
BIDDLES LTD.
Guildford, Surrey

# Contents

The William Salt Library, Stafford

# List of Plates

## Maps and Plans

# Preface

The years since the first edition of *A History of Staffordshire* appeared in 1965 have seen a great change in the study of Staffordshire's history. Its scope has been greatly enlarged by the availability of new raw material, the publication of new books and articles, the appearance of new lines of research, and the establishment of new institutions such as museums and local history societies. To take just the two printed series singled out in the preface to the first edition, the Staffordshire Record Society has issued eight new volumes with a ninth on the way, and the Staffordshire *Victoria County History* has published four more volumes with a fifth due later this year.

As a result the book has had to be rethought. Several chapters have been completely rewritten, the select bibliography has been extended, and the general shape has been recast. In addition the publishers have greatly expanded the visual content. This second edition is largely a new book.

There have been extensive changes in local government boundaries since 1965, notably the formation in 1974 of the new county of West Midlands which includes much of South Staffordshire. Further change is expected in the next few years. While noting the changes, this book is concerned broadly with the geographical county of Staffordshire as it existed before such reorganisation took place.

Many people have helped us in the preparation of the new edition, and we thank them all. We are most grateful to the owners and custodians of the various items used in the illustrations. The drawing of Edward Leigh is reproduced by courtesy of the Trustees of the British Museum; the drawing of the earl of Derby is reproduced by permission of the British Library; the drawing of the pottery figure of Sir Robert Peel is reproduced by courtesy of Oliver-Sutton Antiques; and the plans of Stafford Castle, Main Staffordshire Roads and Staffordshire Forests are based upon Ordnance Survey material, Crown Copyright Reserved.

We also wish to thank the staff of the County Planning and Development Department, especially Ian Boughton, Bob Meeson (who in particular gave advice on chapters II and III), Richard Preston, Ken Sheridan, and Alan Taylor; Freddie Stitt, County Archivist and William Salt Librarian, and his staff, especially Dudley Fowkes and Margaret O'Sullivan at the County Record Office and Cathy Boden at the William Salt Library; Gaye Blake Roberts, curator of the Wedgwood Museum,

Barlaston; Charles Hill, archaeologist with Stafford Borough Council; Douglas Johnson, assistant editor of the Staffordshire *Victoria County History*; and John Rhodes, senior museum officer at the County Museum, Shugborough. Special thanks are due to Barbara Stuart for help with typing and indexing.

*July 1984*                                                                    M.W.G.
                                                                               D.G.S.

*Walsall guildhall in 1867*

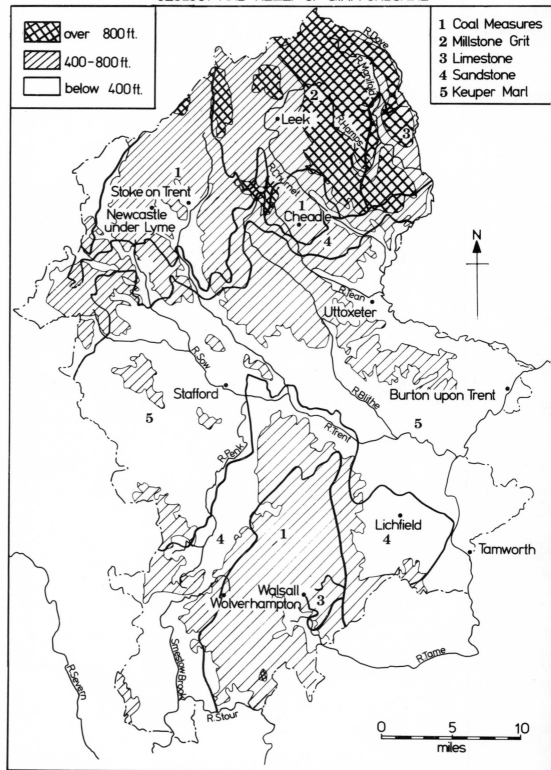

GEOLOGY AND RELIEF OF STAFFORDSHIRE

Legend:
- over 800 ft.
- 400–800 ft.
- below 400 ft.

1 Coal Measures
2 Millstone Grit
3 Limestone
4 Sandstone
5 Keuper Marl

N

Stoke on Trent
Newcastle under Lyme
Leek
Cheadle
Uttoxeter
Burton upon Trent
Stafford
Wolverhampton
Walsall
Lichfield
Tamworth

R. Dove
R. Manifold
R. Hamps
R. Churnet
R. Tean
R. Blithe
R. Sow
R. Penk
R. Trent
R. Severn
Smestow Brook
R. Stour
R. Tame

0        5        10
miles

# I The Setting

England can show nothing more beautiful and nothing uglier than the works of nature and the works of man to be seen within the limits of the county. It is England in little, lost in the midst of England, unsung by searchers after the extreme.

Thus Arnold Bennett, the novelist of the Staffordshire Potteries, evoked his native county in *The Old Wives' Tales*. Today, three-quarters of a century later, Staffordshire retains its natural beauty, which ranges from the limestone gorge of Dovedale, through the lush pastures of the Trent valley, to the sandstone escarpment of Kinver Edge. The man-made industrial landscape, however, has been greatly improved. The Black Country no longer deserves its name. The Potteries lost its smoke pall with the disappearance of the smokey bottle-shaped kilns that characterised its skyline in Bennett's day; the few that remain are much acclaimed museum pieces. Some industrial wasteland has been reclaimed for recreation areas, such as Forest Park in Hanley and Baggeridge country park south of Wolverhampton. In appearance the county is largely as it was shaped in the 18th and 19th centuries, and the contrasts in the Staffordshire scene which caught Bennett's attention remain, reflecting and symbolising much of the county's history.

*Kinver Edge: Holy Austin Rock with former rock houses*

The county, roughly a lozenge in shape, 56 miles long and 38 miles broad at its greatest extent, is divided into three main regions whose history has been influenced by the underlying geological formations and physical configuration. William Camden described the three-fold division concisely in his *Britannia,* first published in 1586: 'The north part is mountainous, and the less fertile; but the middle, which is watered by the Trent, is fruitful, woody and pleasant, by an equal mixture of arable and meadow grounds; so also is the south, which has much pit coal and mines of iron'.

The most northerly of these regions is an extension of the Pennine Chain and is composed of Carboniferous rocks containing the coal-bearing strata of the Potteries and Cheadle coalfields. There is archaeological evidence of coalmining in the area in the second century A.D. The earliest documentary mention is in 1282 when there is a reference to a 'mine of sea coal' in the manor of Tunstall. The Potteries coalfield yielded a quick-burning coal used until recent times in pottery manufacture. The development of the Potteries towns and villages was based on the presence of this coal in conjunction with clay used for making

13

*Clarence Street Maltings,
Burton upon Trent*

coarse earthenware and pottery kilns. The extensive faulting has influenced the economic history of the region. Thus the Apedale Fault interrupts the productive Coal Measures so that Newcastle under Lyme lies in pleasant agricultural country with coalmining districts to the east, north and west. The Blackband ironstones found in the Coal Measures were the basis of the North Staffordshire iron industry. Glacial clays provided the material for brickmaking.

To the east of the Coal Measures lies the Millstone Grit region which produces a dark stone much used for building. The Grit has given rise to distinctive features—high hills like Axe Edge, Brown Edge and Ladderedge, and spectacular outcrops like the Roaches north of Leek, much used by climbers. Further east still lies a limestone region, with the quarry at Caldon Low one of the largest in the area. The rivers Churnet, Hamps, Manifold and Dove have cut deep valleys through the moorland district, and Dovedale is a favourite resort for tourists.

Physically, the northern region consists of a series of elongated plateaux running in a south-easterly direction. The ridge to the west of the Potteries has made communications with Chester and Liverpool more difficult than those with the south and east. This feature influenced the development of roads, canals and railways in the area during its early industrialisation. In the Moorlands of the north-east the plateaux are mostly some 800 feet above sea level, but occasionally rise much higher. Flash, at an altitude of 1,518 feet, claims to be the highest village in England. The elevation of the Moorlands makes for long, hard winters: Camden described the area as 'so rugged, foul, and cold that the snows continue long undissolved, so that concerning a country village here called Wotton, seated at the bottom of Wever Hill, the neighbours have this rhyme among them, "Wotton under Wever, where God came never"'. The bareness of the bleak heathy landscape has been enhanced by tree-felling and the action of sheep and rabbits.

The central region of the county is formed of rocks of the Triassic period, mostly Keuper red marls. They have provided the basis for a fertile soil, though Staffordshire is primarily a dairy-farming rather than an arable county. The sandstones of the region are used for building, and the stone for the rebuilt Coventry cathedral, consecrated in 1962, was quarried at Hollington. Valuable deposits of gypsum are found near Burton upon Trent. Springs rising through beds of gypsum produce a hard water suitable for brewing beer, an industry for which the town has long been noted. Gypsum in its compact form of alabaster is quarried at Fauld, near Tutbury, and was formerly used for sculptured work on ornamental tombs. The clay of the central region was used for making bricks in the Lichfield area by the late 15th century.

14

The area is drained by the river Trent and its tributaries. The downward gradient of the Trent flattens out after Stone and the region is prone to flooding. The name Trent derives from a Celtic word meaning 'trespasser' and thus suggests a river liable to flood. Such flooding produces excellent grassland. Stafford, the county town in the centre of the county, is sited on glacier-borne gravels amid the marshes of the river Sow. Cattle grazing on the fertile river plains provided the leather on which the town's boot and shoe industry developed. Until the later 18th century the central region was the richest part of the county and contained most of the population; besides Stafford, the towns of Stone, Rugeley, Lichfield and Tamworth lie here. Staffordshire's rivers are not, however, navigable for commercial purposes, and this fact contributed to the relative isolation of the county in earlier times.

The third region of the county, in the south, is dominated by the South Staffordshire Plateau. This includes a wedge-shaped Carboniferous uplift, 23 miles long by six miles wide at its greatest extent, with its point near Brereton, south of Rugeley, and its base in Worcestershire. On the productive Coal Measures of the region the Cannock Chase and South Staffordshire coalfields developed. Coal was being dug on Cannock Chase as early as 1298. There the seams of coal are thin, and much of the area is covered by glacial drift which overlaid the coal-bearing outcrops. It was not until the mid-19th century that major expansion of coalmining in the district began, as the demand from the growing industries of South Staffordshire increased. The first recorded instance of digging for coal in South Staffordshire was at Sedgley in 1273. By the mid-16th century the coal of the area was being used in the forges of Birmingham. That coal was more readily accessible. The Thick Coal consists of 12 to 14 different seams which coalesce to give the appearance of a single bed of coal. It outcrops from Dudley to Darlaston, and elsewhere in the area it is often less than 400 feet below the surface. The coal, in conjunction with ironstone in the Coal Measures, fostered industrial development, and South Staffordshire became one of the greatest manufacturing centres in the world. The visible effects of industrialisation were striking, and the area became known as the Black Country in the 19th century. A visitor about 1840 provided a vivid picture of the landscape: 'The traveller appears never to get out of an interminable village, composed of cottages and very ordinary houses . . . interspersed with blazing furnaces, heaps of burning coal in process of coking, piles of ironstone calcining, forges, pit-banks and engine chimneys'.

Physically the Plateau is divided by the rivers Tame and Stour into four upland areas, of which Cannock Chase and the Sedgley–Northfield

*Boys and pit ponies at Bradley colliery near Bilston in the earlier 19th century*

Ridge lie within Staffordshire. North of the Tame the land rises at Barr Beacon to 700 feet, and at Castle Ring, near Cannock, to 801 feet. The northern part of Cannock Chase has been taken over by Staffordshire county council and preserved as an area of natural beauty. South of the Tame the Sedgley–Northfield Ridge rises to 876 feet at Turner's Hill, south-east of Dudley. It is a barrier to easy communications with the valley of the river Severn to the south-west, and thus furthered a physical and economic expansion south-east to Birmingham. West of the ridge the Stour and its tributaries form deep valleys as they drain towards the Severn, and their gradients provided water power for the early iron industry.

Such is the natural setting for the history of Staffordshire and its people. Unnavigable rivers and large tracts of forest, marsh and moorland hindered the early development of the county. From the mid-18th century improvement in communications, hand in hand with technological advances, made it possible for the inhabitants of the county to exploit their rich endowment of mineral resources. The result was an increase in prosperity and an explosion of population. The census of 1801 recorded the population of Staffordshire as 242,693; by 1901 it had risen five-fold to 1,234,533.

The county's geographical boundaries have remained fairly stable since the shire was created in the 10th century. In the north and the east hills and the rivers Dane and Dove provide natural boundaries, but there is no such definition elsewhere. In the 12th century eight manors in the south-west and two a little further north were transferred to Shropshire. Thereafter there were no changes until the first modern boundary revision in 1844. In that year Clent and Broom, two enclaves in Worcestershire, were transferred to that county. The parish of Dudley, also belonging to Worcestershire since at least the time of Domesday Book, was left untouched; Dudley castle and priory were declared to be in Staffordshire by papal decree in 1238. There were further adjustments in the late 19th century in the south and east of the county. Further changes in the 20th century culminated in the reorganisation of 1974 when the county lost the Black Country to the newly created county of West Midlands.

Within this administrative setting the people of Staffordshire have fashioned their history. The role and importance of some of the local leaders—peers, gentry, churchmen, industrial and commercial entrepreneurs—are outlined later in this book. The county is also associated with many nationally famous figures. Izaak Walton (1593–1688), author of *The Compleat Angler* (1653), was born at Stafford and fished the rivers of Staffordshire, being particularly associated with Dovedale. Beside Meece brook at Shallowford stands a small half-timbered

*Izaak Walton*

16

The Roaches near Leek about 1840. From a watercolour drawing by L.J. Wood. (*William Salt Library, Stafford.*)

2. Castle Ring, the Iron Age hillfort on Cannock Chase, from the north in 1948. The picture also shows Forestry Commission plantations. (*Photograph by J.K. St Joseph; University of Cambridge.*)

3. Sir William Paget, later Baron Paget. An engraving from a painting by Hans Holbein. (*William Salt Library.*)

4. Hervey Bagot of Blithfield and his son Hervey in 16 (*Lady Bagot and English Life Publications Ltd.*)

5. Tamworth Castle from the south. Engraving of 1832 from a drawing by J.M.W. Turner. (*William Salt Library.*)

6.   Trentham Hall from the south-west about 1680. (*R. Plot*, The Natural History of Staffordshire, *1686.*)

7.   Trentham Hall from the south-west in 1846. Lithotint by F.W. Hulme. (*William Salt Library.*)
8.   Keele Hall from the south-west about 1680. (*Plot*, Staffordshire.)

9. Shugborough from the south-west about 1800. Based on a drawing by Stebbing Shaw.(*William Salt Library*.)

10. The Bishop's Palace, Lichfield, from the south-east in 1833. Drawing by J. Buckler.(*William Salt Library*.)

building, once owned by Walton and now a museum to his memory. A notable Staffordshire figure of the mid-18th century is Admiral George Anson (1697-1762), a younger son of the Ansons of Shugborough; his circumnavigation of the world from 1740 to 1744 brought him fame, wealth, and a barony. Dr. Samuel Johnson (1709-84) was born in Lichfield. His *Dictionary,* published in 1755, is a landmark in English literary history. Johnson's memorial in the market place of Lichfield shows him sitting ponderously in his chair, facing the house where he was born. In Uttoxeter market place is another monument marking the scene of his penance as a man for having refused as a boy to help on his father's bookstall. David Garrick (1717-79), the actor, grew up in Lichfield and was briefly taught by Johnson, in whose company he left for London in 1737.

*Dr. Johnson's birthplace, Lichfield*

Mary Ann Evans (1819-80), who wrote under the pen-name of George Eliot, was the daughter of Robert Evans who in his youth lived at Ellastone near Rocester. The village provides the setting for her novel *Adam Bede,* and her father was the model for Adam. The author Rudyard Kipling was named after Rudyard Lake near Leek, where his parents first met in 1863. His father was John Lockwood Kipling, an architectural sculptor who helped design the Wedgwood Memorial Institute in Burslem; his mother was Alice MacDonald, whose sisters included Georgiana, wife of Edward Burne-Jones, the painter, and Louisa, mother of the statesman Stanley Baldwin. Among other literary figures associated with Staffordshire Arnold Bennett (1867-1931) is outstanding; most of his best-known novels are set in the Potteries towns, with characters based on local people whom he had known in his early years. Peter de Wint (1784-1849), the landscape painter, was born at Stone, the son of a physician descended from a Dutch family.

Josiah Wedgwood (1730-95), dealt with in detail later, produced pottery which has been internationally famous for more than 200 years. Sir Robert Peel (1788-1850) came of a Lancashire family which established cotton mills at Burton upon Trent, Tamworth and Fazeley in the late 18th century, making its home at Drayton Bassett, near Tamworth. Sir Robert Peel was prime minister in 1834-5 and 1841-6; his pronouncement of 1834 on Conservative attitudes to reform, known as the Tamworth Manifesto, marked an important stage in English party political history. S. F. Barnes (1873-1967), a native of Smethwick, was a Test and county cricketer and one of the greatest bowlers in English cricket. Sir Stanley Matthews, born at Hanley in 1915, is the first footballer to have been knighted while still a player; a brilliant outside-right, he became known as 'the wizard of dribble'. Madeleine Carroll, who was born in West Bromwich in 1906, was a film star of the 1930s and 1940s; her films include *The Prisoner of Zenda* and *The Thirty Nine Steps.*

*Madeleine Carroll*

17

# II  Prehistoric and Roman Times

*Thor's Cave*

The discovery of two Palaeolithic axes at Shenstone and Drayton Bassett, in the south-east of the county, suggests that human settlement in the area may pre-date the last Ice Age, which lasted approximately from 26,000 to 15,000 B.C. Evidence of settlement after the ice had retreated dates from about 9000 B.C.; flint and bone tools have been found in a number of caves in the Manifold Valley in the north-east, including Ossum's Cave, Thor's Cave and Thor's Fissure. The caves went on being occupied during the Mesolithic period, which is dated approximately from 9000 to 4500 B.C. This period is best represented in Staffordshire, however, by flint implements found at Bourne Pool near Aldridge in the south-east.

In the Neolithic period, from about 4500 to 2000 B.C., men learned how to cultivate wheat and barley and make stone axes capable of felling trees. Examples of such tools have been found all over the county. The most striking visible remains of the Neolithic Age, however, are the barrows (or burial mounds). At Mucklestone in the west there are two stones called the Devil's Ring and Finger, which once formed part of a chambered tomb intended for collective burial. At Long Low near Wetton, east of Leek, there are two round barrows linked by a bank, an arrangement not found elsewhere in England. Nearly 200 round barrows have been located in Staffordshire; many, intended initially for single interment, have secondary inhumations and cremations. The concentration of barrows in the north-east of the county reflects the accident of survival; many burial mounds elsewhere in the county have been destroyed by ploughing or have disappeared beneath industrial sites.

The Beaker cultures of the early Bronze Age, from about 2000 to 1300 B.C., are so called because of finds of beakers or drinking mugs of a distinctive form of decoration. Examples have been discovered in the north-east at Alstonefield, Blore, Grindon and Ilam. On hills near Wetton are burial sites which include containers for food and are thought to belong to a people whose culture is called Food Vessel. In the Bronze Age, which lasted to approximately 600 B.C., cremation gradually replaced burial of the dead, and there are numerous barrows in Staffordshire with evidence of this practice. Palstaves (bronze axes fitted into wooden handles) have been found all over the county. Two bracelets from Thorswood House Farm in the parish of Stanton on the

18

north-eastern edge of the county and a gold torc or necklace found at Pattingham in the south-west, also date from the Bronze Age.

Staffordshire may have been subject to Celtic influence from about 250 B.C. It was part of an area inhabited by the Cornovii, whose tribal capital was later established by the Romans at Wroxeter. Tribal boundaries are uncertain; the south-east of the county may have been held by another tribe, the Coritani, and the north-east by the Brigantes. Little is known about the Cornovii, and Iron Age remains are scanty except for hill forts, of which nine are known in the county—Bunbury Hill near Alton, Berth Hill near Maer, Bury Bank north of Darlaston near Stone, Marchington near Uttoxeter, Berry Ring near Stafford, Castle Ring on Cannock Chase, Castle Old Fort near Brownhills, Bishop's Wood near Eccleshall, and Kinver Edge in the south-west corner of the county. Castle Ring is the largest and most elaborate of these hill forts, standing at 801 feet on the highest point of Cannock Chase, nine acres in extent and fortified with banks and ditches.

*Bronze Age cup found at Stanshope in the Moorlands*

More evidence exists for Staffordshire's history in the Roman period. In A.D. 48 Publius Ostorius Scapula, the second Roman governor of Britain, advanced through the Midlands and established a forward base at Letocetum, the modern Wall near Lichfield. Eventually the greater part of the territory of the Cornovii was brought under Roman control. A number of Roman roads pass through Staffordshire. Watling Street, mainly the modern A5, entered the county at Fazeley near Tamworth and ran north-west to Letocetum and Pennocrucium to leave the county just beyond Weston under Lizard. Letocetum, which is a corrupt and Latinised form of a Celtic word meaning 'grey wood', was an important Romano-British settlement. It was first used as a marching camp and was later the site of a number of first-century forts. About A.D. 80 a general pacification of the area allowed a civil administration to be set up, and the military fort was abandoned. Fresh defences were built at the end of the third century A.D., probably to make the settlement one of the strong points along Watling Street established to restore Roman control over the troubled province of Britain. Little is known about the civil settlement at Wall. There the traveller could obtain not only a change of horses (*mutatio*), but also overnight accommodation (*mansio*). The settlement included a bath house, built of local stone, with the usual suite of rooms of different temperatures. Recent excavations have revealed evidence for the existence there in the first century A.D. of a pagan Celtic shrine. A number of carved stones, some with horned human heads, have been found. Wall may have been a religious sanctuary of the Cornovii, whose name may mean 'Worshippers of the Horned One'. Some of the stones have been inserted upside-down in a wall. One explanation of this is

19

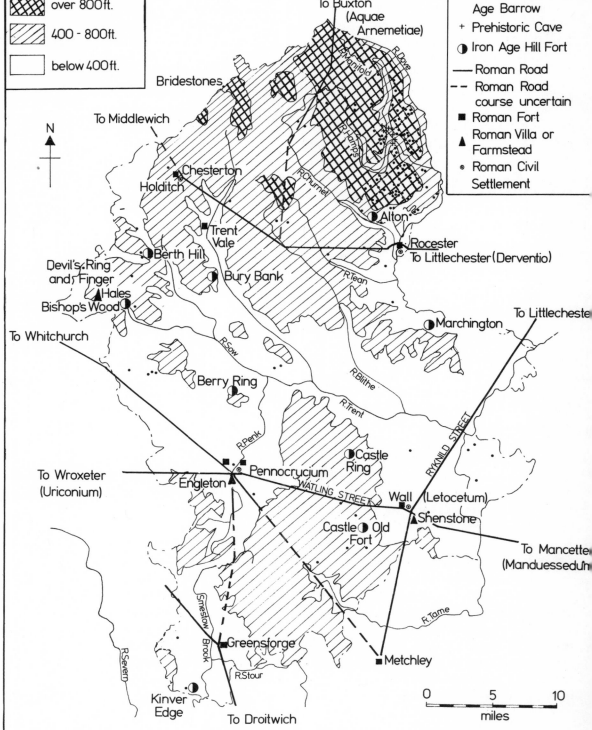

## STAFFORDSHIRE IN PREHISTORIC AND ROMAN TIMES

**Legend:**
- ⬜ over 800 ft.
- ⬜ 400 – 800 ft.
- ⬜ below 400 ft.

- • Neolithic or Bronze Age Barrow
- + Prehistoric Cave
- ◗ Iron Age Hill Fort
- — Roman Road
- – – Roman Road course uncertain
- ■ Roman Fort
- ▲ Roman Villa or Farmstead
- ⊚ Roman Civil Settlement

N

To Buxton (Aquae Arnemetiae)

Bridestones

To Middlewich

Chesterton
Holditch

Trent Vale

Berth Hill

Devil's Ring and Finger
Hales
Bishop's Wood

To Whitchurch

Bury Bank

Alton

Rocester
To Littlechester (Derventio)

R.Manifold
R.Dove
R.Hamps
R.Churnet
R.Tean

Marchington

To Littlechester

Berry Ring

R.Sow

R.Blithe

R.Trent

R.Penk

Castle Ring

RYKNILD STREET

To Wroxeter (Uriconium)

Engleton
Pennocrucium

WATLING STREET

Wall (Letocetum)
Shenstone

Castle Old Fort

To Mancetter (Manduessedum)

R.Tame

Smestow Brook

Greensforge

R.Severn

R.Stour

Metchley

Kinver Edge

To Droitwich

0    5    10
miles

that the Romans destroyed the shrine but preserved some stones, hoping to guard against the hostility of the deity while not entirely alienating it. The remains of Celtic oxen with turned-down horns (*bos longiflons*) have also been found in the area, and they may represent the sacrificial killing and eating of horned beasts.

*Celtic carved stone of the first century A.D. from Wall, perhaps showing warriors and water deities*

Twelve miles west of Wall on Watling Street was Pennocrucium, a name of Celtic origin meaning 'chief mound'. Pennocrucium may have been a centre for Celtic religious gatherings. Excavation there has revealed a complex of enclosures which in Roman times included forts and a civil settlement. Watling Street was joined there by two roads coming from the south and a third coming from the north-west. Pottery found on the site lies within the period A.D. 50 to 200. The civil settlement was occupied throughout the Roman period.

The other important road in Staffordshire was Ryknild Street, which crossed Watling Street half a mile south-east of Wall. Its route through Staffordshire is followed and paralleled by the modern A38. From its junction with Watling Street it ran north-east to Burton upon Trent, crossing the river Dove, the county boundary, near Clay Mills. Two Romano-British farmsteads have been discovered at Shenstone and Fisherwick, close to Ryknild Street, and this has led to the suggestion that the valleys of the Trent and the Tame were extensively farmed in the Roman period.

Another Roman road, also called Ryknild Street in medieval times, entered what later became Staffordshire at Rocester, ran west towards Chesterton and then continued across the county boundary and on towards Chester. The Roman settlement at Rocester covered several successive sites. The early pottery there dates from A.D. 60 to 100, and it has been suggested that the first fort may have been built about A.D. 69 during the pacification of the area by Agricola. Military occupation ceased about A.D. 120 and the Rocester area passed into civil administration. Defences for the civil settlement were added about A.D. 160, and again about A.D. 280.

Chesterton is the most important Roman site in the north-west of the county. Sampson Erdeswick, the first historian of the county, wrote, about 1600, of 'ruins of a very ancient town . . . the walls have been of a marvellous thickness'. The ruins may have been the remains of a fort of the last quarter of the first century A.D. which was occupied only for a short period. To the east there was a settlement at Holditch, occupied from the late first to the third century A.D. and probably supporting the military garrison. The artisan population worked metal and exploited the local raw materials—clay, ironstone, and coal. About five miles south-east of Chesterton at Trent Vale a Roman kiln has been discovered with pottery dating from the third quarter of the first century A.D.

21

The number of Roman villas so far discovered in Staffordshire—and indeed in the territory of the Cornovii as a whole—is small. At Hales in the parish of Tyrley, about 12 miles south-west of Chesterton, excavations have revealed evidence of the existence of a corridor villa possibly dating from the late first century and of a bath-house possibly built in the first half of the second century. At Engleton in the parish of Brewood, close to Pennocrucium, another corridor villa with bath wing has been investigated, the pottery finds suggesting an occupation from the second to the fourth century A.D.

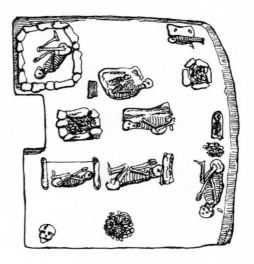

*Barrow at Top Low, Swinscoe*

# III  The Anglo-Saxon Period

Anglian invaders first settled in Staffordshire in the later sixth century. It has been suggested that the invaders came from two directions. One group, coming from the Wash westwards into the Midlands, may have entered South Staffordshire along the line of Watling Street. Other groups may have come from the Humber estuary along the line of the river Trent. Near Burton upon Trent there is a concentration of Anglian sites which suggests much settlement in the area—unless these findings are the chance result of the volume of canal and railway building and gravel extraction. Excavations at Stapenhill, Burton upon Trent, have revealed a large cemetery with traces of 36 burials. Two were cremations, a pagan practice which continued until the conversion of the Anglo-Saxons to Christianity in the seventh century. Further up the Trent at Wychnor is another site containing only remains of inhumation burials. At nearby Catholme there was a large Anglian settlement, where the ground-plans of 66 buildings have been revealed. The site may represent the development of five or seven farmsteads over the period between the late fifth and early 10th centuries. The eventual abandonment of the site may have been caused by the Danish invasions which began in the late ninth century: the element -holme in the place-name Catholme is of Danish origin. Some of the Anglian invaders turned north up the Dove valley. There are burial sites in the north-east of the county at Ramshorn, Blore, Waterhouses and Alstonefield. The Dove valley people may have been members of the Pecsaetan, a folk centred on the Peak District of Derbyshire.

The tribal identity of the earliest Anglian arrivals has not been firmly established. It has been suggested that they were members of the Middle Anglian group of peoples, which included the Bilsaetan, centred on Bilston, and the Tamsaetan, the people of the Tame. Staffordshire became part of Mercia, a word derived from the Mierce, who were the people of the march or border between the English and the British. Wychnor means the slope or bank of the Hwicce, whose tribal area extended to Gloucestershire. The origin of the name Hwicce is uncertain; it may be Celtic, and the Hwicce may have been a British people. Archaeological evidence suggests that the Anglian invaders stopped near Lichfield for some time and that the district around Lichfield was part of the boundary area between the English and British. The invaders met with at least one defeat in the area: a Welsh

*Anglian brooch found at Wychnor*

23

poem of the period deals with the exploits of Cynddylan, a prince of Powys, who was allied to Morfael, a Celtic leader in the Lichfield area. Together they defeated the English in battle at Caer Luitcoet, identified as Wall, about A.D. 655.

There was probably no wholesale massacre by the newcomers of the British inhabitants. There is, indeed, some evidence of cultural inter-mixing: a burial site at Barlaston, near the Trent south of the Potteries, shows both Anglian and Celtic features. Although the majority of the county's place-names are of English origin, there are some, such as Cannock, Eccleshall, Kinver, Penkhull, Penn, Walton, and Walsall, of Celtic derivation.

Whether any British Christianity survived in Staffordshire is uncertain. The name Eccleshall is taken to mean the existence of a Christian community in the later Romano-British period. The Welsh poem about Cynddylan mentions bishops and monks among the enemy attacked at Wall. The earliest Anglo-Saxons were pagans. Woden, the god of war and poetry, was worshipped in South Staffordshire, where Wednesbury and Wednesfield commemorate his name. The accepted date for the beginning of the conversion of the English to Christianity in Staffordshire is A.D. 653. In that year Peada, sub-king of the Middle Angles, accepted Christianity so that he might marry the daughter of Oswiu, the Christian king of Northumbria. Peada brought back four missionaries from Northumbria who began working in Mercia. All the early evangelists in Staffordshire were Celtic born or Celtic trained. The most famous of them was St Chad, a monk from Northumbria who had been a disciple of St Aidan. Chad was appointed bishop of the Mercians in 669 and established his centre at Lichfield, continuing the conversion of the area until his death from plague in 672. Wulfhere, who was king of Mercia from 659 to 674, endowed the bishopric with lands. Wulfhere is also said to have founded a monastery at Stone, but there is no foundation for the story that he adopted Christianity in remorse for having slain his two sons after their conversion by Chad. In 788, under Offa, king of Mercia from 757 to 796, Lichfield was raised to the status of an archbishopric, but after Offa's death it was reduced to its former status. In 822 Bishop Ethelweald established a cathedral chapter of 20 canons under a provost.

Wulfhere's daughter, Werburgh, was abbess of a nunnery at Hanbury. The fate of the community there is recorded in a charter of the abbey of St Werburgh at Chester: St Werburgh died at Hanbury in 700, and her body is said to have remained incorrupt until 874 when it crumbled away lest it fall into the hands of the invading Danes; the nuns fled to Chester, carrying the saint's relics with them. Another monastic foundation, possibly of the seventh century, was at Burton upon Trent,

*Disc from an Anglian enamelled bowl with Celtic features found at Barlaston*

24

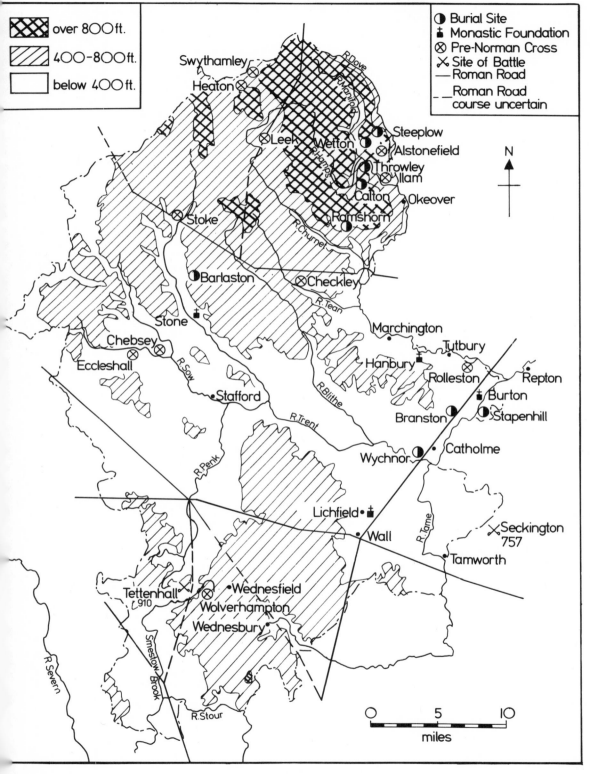

# STAFFORDSHIRE IN THE ANGLO-SAXON PERIOD

over 800 ft.

400-800 ft.

below 400 ft.

◑ Burial Site
⚲ Monastic Foundation
⊗ Pre-Norman Cross
✕ Site of Battle
— Roman Road
-- Roman Road course uncertain

N

Swythamley
Heaton ⊗
R.Dove
R.Manifold
⊗ Leek
Wetton
Steeplow
⊗ Alstonefield
Throwley
Ilam ⊗
Calton
Okeover
⊗ Stoke
R.Churnet
Ramshorn
R.Hamps

◑ Barlaston
⊗ Checkley

R.Tean
Stone ⚲

Marchington
Tutbury

Chebsey ⊗
R.Sow
Hanbury
Rolleston ⊗
Repton

Eccleshall
R.Blithe
⚲ Burton
Stafford
Branston ◑
◑ Stapenhill

R.Trent
Wychnor ◑
• Catholme

R.Penk
Lichfield • ⚲
✕ Seckington
757
R.Tame
Wall
Tamworth

Tettenhall
✕ 910
⊗ • Wednesfield
Wolverhampton
Wednesbury

R.Severn
Smestow Brook
R.Stour

○      5      10
miles

*Silver pennies of Athelstan from the Tamworth mint*

where an Irish abbess, St Modwen, is said to have founded a community on an island in the river Trent called Andressey, evidently because the church was dedicated to St Andrew. The Danish invasions of the later ninth century probably put an end to surviving monasteries in the county.

Mercia grew to be the largest and most powerful of the Anglo-Saxon kingdoms. Its heartland lay in the valleys of the Trent and the Tame, and Offa built a palace at Tamworth. Eventually the rivalry of other English kingdoms and the Danish invasions, which reached Staffordshire in 874, put an end to Mercia's political supremacy. From their base at Repton the Danes subdued the whole of the surrounding countryside and destroyed Tamworth. Their advance was checked by Alfred, king of Wessex, and by the Treaty of Wedmore (878) Danish authority was more or less confined to the area north of Watling Street, which became known as the Danelaw. Central and northern Staffordshire thus fell under Danish control. There is little evidence, however, of extensive Scandinavian settlement in the county. A few place-names of Scandinavian origin exist. Thorpe Constantine and Croxall in the south-east of the county are the only certain Scandinavian parish names; some islands in the Trent are called 'holme', a Danish word meaning dry land in a fen or stream. There is an Upper Hulme in the north-east of the county. At Tamworth street names of Danish origin—Aldergate, formerly Ellergate, and Gungate, formerly Gumpegate—survive from a period of Danish occupation.

The Danes renewed their attacks on England south of the Danelaw in the late ninth century, but were checked by Edward the Elder, Alfred's son, at the battle of Tettenhall in 910. Edward's sister Ethelfleda, widow of Ethelred the ealdorman of Mercia, played a prominent part in the reconquest of the Danelaw. She fortified Stafford and Tamworth in 913. She died at Tamworth in 918 and the Mercians submitted to the authority of Edward. During the reign of his son Athelstan (924–39) royal mints were established at Stafford and Tamworth. During a Danish rebellion in 943 against the royal authority Tamworth was attacked and many of its inhabitants massacred. Further Danish incursions took place in the late 10th century, and tradition tells of a massacre of Danes in the neighbourhood of Marchington, north-west of Burton upon Trent, in 1002. Sweyn, king of Denmark, launched a fresh invasion from Denmark in 1013, and Staffordshire, like the rest of Mercia, was ravaged during his advance.

By the 11th century there were numerous churches in Staffordshire, although Anglo-Saxon Christian remains in the county are few. There was a church at Stafford by the 10th century associated with St Bertelin, a legendary Anglo-Saxon saint who had a hermitage at

26

Stafford; the line of the foundations of the medieval church have been marked out on its site at the west end of St Mary's church. Fragments of the church fabric at Ilam have been dated to pre-Norman times, and St Editha's church at Tamworth has traces of a late-Saxon crossing tower. A number of free-standing cross-shafts have been found, some of which may have been preaching crosses erected before churches were built. That at Wolverhampton is the most striking. There seem to have been several minsters, central churches from which groups of priests served the surrounding area. One such minster was Lichfield cathedral, and the episcopal estates around Lichfield and Eccleshall may originally have been the area served by the minster priests. The later collegiate churches at Penkridge, Stafford, Tamworth, Tettenhall and Wolverhampton and the semi-collegiate church at Gnosall probably originated as minsters in the 10th or 11th centuries. Parochial organisation was developing at the time of the Conquest, but how far it had advanced by then is not certain. Monastic revival in the county began in the early 11th century when Wulfric Spot, an Anglo-Saxon thegn, in his will made between 1002 and 1004 endowed a Benedictine monastery at Burton upon Trent.

The establishment of Staffordshire as an administrative unit is usually dated to the early 10th century, during the reign of Edward the Elder (899–925). The county was centred on the 'burh' of Stafford built by Ethelfleda on an existing settlement in 913. At the time of Domesday Book the shire was rated for tax at 500 hides, a figure which suggests a relatively poor and undeveloped county. There was a further sub-division into five hundreds, Cuttlestone, Offlow, Pirehill, Seisdon, and Totmonslow. The names derive from prominent topographical features—Pirehill, for example, being a hill south of Stone. At the hundred court taxation was levied, arrangements were made for maintenance of peace and order, and some criminal and civil offences were dealt with. The hundred as an administrative division is probably as old as the county itself. In time the functions of the hundred dwindled as other organs of local government developed, but it retained some residual powers as late as the 19th century.

*Remains of an Anglo-Saxon cross at St Edward's church, Leek*

# IV  The Norman Conquest

*Norman font at Bradley near Stafford*

When the Norman invaders won the battle of Hastings in 1066, England became subject to a new king and a new ruling class. William, duke of Normandy, gained a crown for himself; his followers expected their reward too in the shape of lands and high office in Church and State. William proceeded to establish his power and that of his followers throughout the kingdom with typical Norman efficiency. A picture of the thoroughness with which that was done is given by Domesday Book, the survey of the kingdom which William carried out in 1086 after 20 years of Norman rule.

William is known to have come twice to Staffordshire, each time as a conqueror. The first occasion was in 1069 when the county had joined a rebellion against him. A battle was fought at Stafford, and William defeated the rebels. That was not enough to stamp out resistance in the area, and early the next year William was back. To impress his power on the conquered people he ravaged a great area of Yorkshire and then crossed to Chester, harrying the countryside as he went; Staffordshire was included in his revenge. The destruction was so great that, according to one chronicler, a huge crowd of old men, young men, women and children wandered as far south as the abbey of Evesham in search of food. To make doubly sure that there would be no more trouble in the Stafford area William built a castle there in 1070, probably at Broad Eye on the north-west side of the town. The royal power was so well established that it was not necessary to maintain the castle for long. Domesday Book shows that by 1086 the building, almost certainly a wooden structure, had been allowed to fall into ruin.

William also became the most important landowner in the county. In the first place he inherited the royal manors which had belonged to Edward the Confessor, such as Kingswinford and Penkridge. He also added others, notably most of the manors which had belonged to the earls of Mercia, such as Kinver, Uttoxeter and Leek. Four of William's followers were given much of the remaining land in the county—Roger of Montgomery, earl of Shrewsbury, Henry de Ferrers, Robert de Stafford, and William FitzAnsculf. Those tenants in chief of the king in turn sub-let many of their estates, often to their own followers. A Norman priest, Peter, became bishop of Lichfield in 1072 after the resignation two years before of the Anglo-Saxon Bishop

*Norman font at Ilam*

28

Leofwine, who was in trouble for being a married man with a family: Norman efficiency included religious reform. The extensive episcopal estates thus passed into Norman hands.

The most important Staffordshire landowner in 1086 after the king was Robert de Stafford. He was a younger son of Roger de Toeni, William the Conqueror's standard bearer, and he is a good example of those who made their fortunes in England as followers of William. He was given extensive estates in the Midlands, and it is significant that he took a new family name, de Stafford, for the centre of his power lay in a group of lands west of the county town. A symbol of the family's power is the castle on a hill west of Stafford which, although dating from the early 19th century, occupies the site of a castle built probably by Robert himself. A village lay below the castle, possibly the place called Monetville in Domesday Book; it was abandoned about 1450, but its church of St Mary survives in the place now known as Castle Church.

There was another castle at Tutbury, held by Henry de Ferrers. A town grew up in the shelter of the castle, and by 1086 it had become a market town with 42 merchants resident there. The livelihood of the traders probably depended on the supplying of the castle and of the nearby estates of Henry de Ferrers.

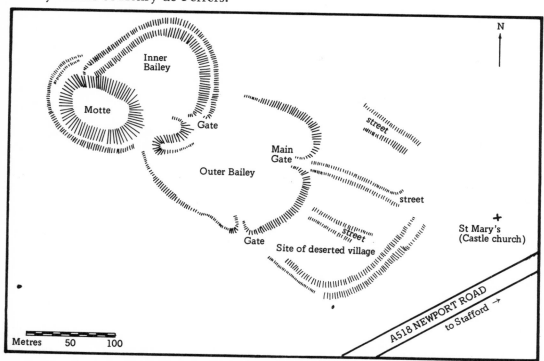

*The site of Stafford Castle and an adjoining deserted village, possibly the Domesday Monetville*

*Stourton Castle in the 1790s*

A further important element in Norman society was the forest. It was not necessarily an area of trees but rather a tract of country strictly preserved as a royal hunting ground with a hierarchy of officials to look after it. In Staffordshire William I enlarged the area of forest—if he did not create it—and much of the county was given over to forest in the Middle Ages. The most important forests there were the two which took their names from Cannock and Kinver. Cannock forest occupied a wide area in the centre of the county extending from Radford bridge near Stafford in the north to Wolverhampton and Walsall in the south and from the river Penk on the west to the Tame on the east. William II visited it, and Henry I on one occasion breakfasted with a tenant at King's Bromley while on his way to hunt in the forest. In the later 1150s Henry II replaced a hunting lodge at Cannock with a new one at Radmore near the present village of Cannock Wood. Wolves still roamed the forest in the 1280s. In 1290 Bishop Meuland was granted a large area around his manors of Cannock and Rugeley. That area survives as Cannock Chase, but the rest of Cannock forest has long since disappeared. In the present century, however, much of the Chase has again become a forest, planted out by the Forestry Commission.

Kinver forest covered the south-west corner of the county and extended into Worcestershire. William II, Henry II and King John visited it. There seems to have been a hunting lodge near Kinver village before 1100. In the mid 1190s a new one was built above the river Stour at Stourton north-east of the village. It consisted of a hall, a kitchen, a chamber, a gaol for forest offenders, and a fortified gateway, and the whole was surrounded by a palisade 16 feet high; the river was dammed to make a fishpond. The lodge was the home of the hereditary keepers of the forest, and one of them began to fortify it in 1223; the king paid for the work and provided timber from the forest. The house became known as Stourton Castle, and although it has been rebuilt over the centuries, there is still a house of that name on the site.

Another important forest was Needwood in the east of the county. Strictly it was a chase, since it was held by a subject, Henry de Ferrers, and only the king could have a forest. Covering an area between the rivers Trent, Dove and Blithe, it evidently existed as a hunting ground before the Conquest. It remained in the Ferrers family until 1266 and then passed to the earls of Lancaster. When the earls were created dukes in 1351, Needwood forest became part of the duchy of Lancaster. It survived, though covering a shrunken area, until 1802. The Abbots Bromley horn dance, an ancient ritual still performed in the village every September, may be connected with the villagers' former rights in the forest.

*Fallow deer on Cannock Chase*

30

STAFFORDSHIRE
FORESTS

10 miles

Tunstall
Hulton
Shelton
Newcastle
Stoke-upon-Trent
Weston Coyney
Trentham
Barlaston
Stallington
Tittensor
Fulford
Moddershall
N E W
Dods Leigh
Stoke
Painsley
Milwich
Uttoxeter
Yarlett
Sandon
Uttoxeter
Ward
River Dove
Marston
River Sow
Salt
Tutbury
Hopton
Stafford
Tixall
N E E D W O O D
Burton
RADFORD
BRIDGE
River Trent
River Blithe
River Trent
Saredon Brook
Rugeley
Penkridge
Teddesley
Hay
A l r e w a s
H a y
Wheaton
Aston
Rodbaston
Radmore
River Penk
Blymhill
G a i l e y
H a y
Weston
Cannock
Lichfield
Brewood
C A N N O C K
B R E W O O D
Gt Wyrley
H o p w a s
H a y
Tong
C h e s l y n
H a y
O g l e y
H a y
Tamworth
Donington
Codsall
Albrighton
Bilbrook
Bourne (or Black) Brook
River Tame
Whottesley
Drayton Bassett
Tettenhall
Wood
B e n t l e y
H a y
Perton
Wolverhampton
Walsall
Wednesbury
River Tame
K I N V E R
Himley
Bobbington
Chasepool
Hay
Dudley
A s h w o o d
H a y
Stourton
River Severn
Kinver
I v e r l e y
H a y
Stourbridge
Upper
Arley
Hagley
Wolverley
Broom
Kidderminster
Chaddesley
Corbett

////// Forests

\\\ Area of Cannock Chase as
granted to the bishop in 1290

▲ Vills described in the 1300
perambulation of Kinver as
partly or wholly afforested
after 1154

–·– County boundary (modern)

New and Brewood forests are shown as they were before being disafforested in 1204; Cannock and Kinver forests as they were in 1300; and Needwood forest as it was probably by the mid-13th century.

William the Conqueror appointed an Englishman, Richard Chenvin, as keeper of Cannock forest. The fact that such an important office, with the estates in Staffordshire and Warwickshire which went with it, could be held by an Englishman is a sign that the Norman Conquest did not involve the immediate or complete submergence of the native population by the invaders, far-reaching though the changes were. Nor was the redistribution of the land without exceptions. In Staffordshire, certainly, most of the land was taken from the English and given to Normans, and the majority of the previous owners could at best hope only to become tenants of the new masters. On the other hand Domesday Book also shows that it was in the upper levels of society alone that the changes had taken place in Staffordshire. The newcomers probably numbered no more than 300, and in the north especially there still lingered members of a once powerful class of English landowners, the Saxon thegns, of whom Richard Chenvin was the most notable and favoured.

The following extract from Domesday Book deals with Barlaston, south of what is now the Potteries area:

*Gnosall church: the 12th-century transept*

Iſd . R . teñ in *BERNVLVESTONE* dimiđ hidā.7 Helgot de eo. Auguſtin tenuit 7 liƀ hō fuit . Tŕa . ē . vi . caŕ . In dñio . ē una. cū . i . ſeruo . 7 iiii . uiłłi 7 iii . borđ cū . i . caŕ . Ibi . vi . ãc p̃ti . 7 iii . ãc ſiluæ . Valet . xl . ſoliđ.

> The same Robert holds ½ hide in BERNULVESTONE and Helgot from him. Augustine held it and he was a free man. There is land for 6 ploughs. In demesne there is one with 1 slave. There are 4 villeins and 3 bordars with 1 plough. There are there 6 acres of meadow and 3 acres of woodland. It is worth 40s.

It shows the change of ownership after the Conquest from a free man named Augustine to Robert de Stafford. Robert had sub-let to Helgot, who was also his tenant at Bobbington in the south-west of the county. Helgot's descendants remained lords of Barlaston under the overlordship of Robert's descendants for almost 300 years; for much of that time they were also keepers of the royal forest of Kinver and lived at Stourton Castle. Domesday Book shows that in 1086 part of Barlaston manor was in demesne—that is, farmed directly by the lord himself. The rest was worked by the local peasants. In addition to the arable there was meadow and woodland. The manor was worth 40s., among the most valuable of Robert's Staffordshire estates. Seven peasant households were mentioned; with the slave on the demesne, that may have represented a population of something over thirty.

32

*Domesday Book for Staffordshire is now available in modern translation, edited by John Morris, as part of the Phillimore History from the Sources series.

In all, Domesday Book reveals a poor, thinly populated county of some 334 settlements, about one-fifth of them waste. Subsistence agriculture was the normal way of life, and the few towns were of small importance. The rural population mentioned was some 3,100—but the total was actually much larger since that figure consisted mainly of heads of households, whose families were not included in the enumeration. There was a concentration in the south-east along the Trent and the Tame, with the royal manors of Alrewas, Elford, and Clifton Campville among the most prosperous in the county. An indication of the population of the towns is given by the mention of some 128 occupied houses in Stafford, with just over 50 unoccupied, and the mention of 42 traders in Tutbury; there was also passing reference to 12 burgesses in the Staffordshire part of Tamworth—the other part was in Warwickshire where 10 were mentioned. Some 40 churches provided for the spiritual needs of the people, but the parish system had not yet taken full shape. Settlement, although its basic pattern was established, was far from complete.

*Tutbury priory church: the 12th-century west doorway, containing the earliest-known use of alabaster in England*

# V County Families and their Houses

*Humphrey, earl of Stafford (later Duke of Buckingham), his wife and son, from a window formerly in Lichfield cathedral*

In medieval times the baronial families of Staffordshire dominated the local scene as feudal lords with wide tracts of land; their military power, rivalling that of the king, centred on their castles. Gradually their power dwindled, curbed by the growing control of the central government. Much of their local authority passed to the gentry, some of whom were in the course of time ennobled. By the 15th century castles were ceasing to be needed for military purposes and, cold and inconvenient as residences, were being rebuilt or replaced. Some of Staffordshire's stately homes date from the great rebuilding period of the later 16th and early 17th centuries. Others were erected in the 18th century in Classical style or given a neo-Gothic appearance in the 19th century. In the 20th century financial stringency prompted many titled and landed families to sell their estates, and several houses, where a buyer could not be found, have been demolished.

The most notable of the county nobility in the Middle Ages was the family of Stafford. Ralph de Toeni, a Norman knight, assumed the name de Stafford because of the concentration of his lands near the town of that name. The military and administrative talents of his descendants brought them high office and titles. Edmund de Stafford, representing the seventh generation of the family after the Norman founder of the line, was first summoned to parliament as a baron in 1299. His son, Ralph, played a prominent military and diplomatic role in the early period of the Hundred Years' War and was created earl of Stafford in 1351. He came by marriage and inheritance into the estates of the Audley family, whose lands spread from Norfolk through the Midlands to the Welsh border, and into a second inheritance, the Corbet lands in Shropshire. Edmund, 5th earl of Stafford, married Anne Plantagenet, daughter of the duke of Gloucester and widow of the 3rd earl of Stafford, soon after 1392. The marriage brought him part of the large de Bohun estates on the Welsh Marches and in the Midlands. He did not live long to enjoy his increased wealth, being killed at the battle of Shrewsbury in 1403. His widow died in 1438 leaving their son, Humphrey, the 6th earl, one of the wealthiest landowners in England; in 1444 he was created duke of Buckingham. He supported the Yorkist cause and was killed at the battle of Northampton in 1460. His grandson, Henry, the 2nd duke, supported Richard of Gloucester

34

in the latter's successful bid for the throne of England in 1483. Later that year Buckingham rebelled against Richard III; the rising failed, and the duke was executed without trial. His son, Edward, 3rd duke of Buckingham, was executed by Henry VIII on a trumped-up charge of treason, but really because his wealth and royal blood seemed to that monarch to constitute a threat. The dukedom and other titles were forfeited, and although the barony of Stafford was restored in 1547, the family fortunes declined.

The heir to the title in 1637 was described as being 'of a very mean and obscure condition' and surrendered it to Charles I in 1640 in return for £800. The barony and a viscountcy were then given to Sir William Howard, who had married Mary, sister and heiress of Henry, 5th Baron Stafford. Viscount Stafford fell a victim to the anti-Catholic hysteria at the time of the 'Popish Plot' and was beheaded in 1680. His son, Henry, created earl in 1688, was for a few years with James II in exile. The earldom became extinct in 1762, but Sir George Jerningham, who was descended through the female line from the last earl, obtained a revival of the barony in 1824. The Jerninghams, too, died out, and in 1913 the title passed to Francis Edward Fitzherbert of Swynnerton, who became 12th Baron Stafford. The 14th baron still lives at Swynnerton about 10 miles north of Stafford in a house built in 1725, probably by Francis Smith of Warwick.

*William Howard, Viscount Stafford, painted by Sir Anthony Van Dyck probably in the late 1630s*

Stafford Castle, long a seat of the Stafford family, is now undergoing major excavation. The castle began in the 11th century with a motte and two baileys. A stone keep was erected in the 12th or 13th century, and about 1350 the whole castle was rebuilt in stone by Ralph, 1st earl of Stafford. Its strength was tested as late as 1643 when Lady Stafford, widow of Edward, Lord Stafford, conducted an energetic defence against besieging parliamentary troops. The castle was eventually abandoned, and the parliamentary committee at Stafford ordered its destruction. The ruins were cleared away in the early 19th century by Sir George Jerningham, the claimant to the Stafford barony. He began the reconstruction of the keep in Gothic Revival style, but it was never finished. The Jerninghams, and later their caretakers, occupied the completed east wing, and timber buildings were added in the 19th century. The castle fell into ruins and was abandoned as a residence in 1949.

Seven miles north-east of Stafford, beside the main road from Stafford to Uttoxeter, stand the impressive ruins of Chartley Castle. The original castle, built by Ranulph de Gernon, earl of Chester, and probably made of wood, was in existence by 1153. On the death of his grandson Ranulph de Blundeville, earl of Chester, in 1232, it passed to William de Ferrers, 4th earl of Derby, who had married

*Remains of Chartley castle*

35

*Tutbury castle: the 15th-century north tower*

Ranulph's sister, Agnes. The castle was rebuilt in stone in the early 13th century, with a motte and two baileys. It was immensely strong, its defences including a keep and five circular towers. In 1461 it passed by marriage to Walter Devereux, created Baron Ferrers in that year. Already the castle had been abandoned as a residence, and Chartley Hall, a moated and battlemented timber mansion, built nearby. When the antiquary John Leland saw the castle about 1540, it was in ruins. Elizabeth I was entertained at Chartley Hall in 1575 on her progress through Staffordshire, when she also stayed at Stafford Castle and Chillington. Mary Queen of Scots was imprisoned at Chartley from December 1585 to September 1586 before being taken to Fotheringhay Castle in Northamptonshire for trial and execution. Robert Devereux, 2nd earl of Essex, became Elizabeth's favourite. He developed political ambitions and sought to further them by building up a clientele in the House of Commons; he was able to nominate six of the county's 10 members of parliament in 1592. A foolish attempt at rebellion in 1601 led to his execution on 25 February in that year, and the forfeiture of his earldom. His son, Robert, was restored in title as 3rd earl on the accession of James I in 1603 and became parliamentary commander-in-chief during the Civil War. He died childless in 1646, and Chartley passed eventually to Sir Robert Shirley, the grandson and heir of Dorothy, the 3rd earl's sister. Shirley was created Baron Ferrers in 1677 and Earl Ferrers in 1711. Chartley Hall was destroyed by fire in 1781, and the present house was built in an Elizabethan style in 1847.

The Ferrers family also owned Tutbury Castle for a time. Its splendid natural site had marked it out for habitation and defence in the Anglo-Saxon period. The early history of the building is obscure, but there are earth ramparts and a ditch dating from the early Norman period. William the Conqueror gave Tutbury to Henry de Ferrers in 1071, and it became the administrative centre of Henry's widespread holding of over 200 manors, largely in Derbyshire. He used Tutbury as his principal residence and also founded a Benedictine priory below the castle. His descendant William, 3rd earl of Derby, rebelled against Henry II, and the castle was demolished in 1175–6. It was rebuilt late in the 12th century and the wooden keep was replaced by one of stone. It was again demolished in 1322, after the rebellion of Thomas, earl of Lancaster, against Edward II. It was rebuilt once more in the mid 14th century, and there were extensive additions in the 15th century. Edward III gave Tutbury to his fourth son, John of Gaunt, who was created duke of Lancaster in 1362. He held a splendid court in the castle in the later 14th century. Since 1399, when Henry, duke of Lancaster, came to the throne as Henry IV, Tutbury has belonged to the sovereign as part of the duchy of Lancaster. By the 16th century

36

the castle had fallen into disrepair, and Mary Queen of Scots, who was imprisoned there on four occasions between 1569 and 1585, complained bitterly about the dampness of her accommodation. She was also offended by the continual stench from the privy below her window. In 1643 the castle was garrisoned by royalist troops, and after its surrender in 1646 parliament ordered its destruction. The demolition was not completed, and after the Restoration, some of the rooms were repaired. It was leased in 1681 to the Vernon family of nearby Sudbury Hall in Derbyshire. Some time in the last quarter of the 18th century Lord Vernon erected an artificial ruin in the form of a keep on the inner mound to improve the view from Sudbury. In the early 19th century part of the south range of the castle was used as a farmhouse and farm buildings were added. The castle finally ceased to be used as a farm in 1952, and is now preserved by the duchy of Lancaster as an historic monument.

*Alton Towers: the Armoury Tower*

Alton Castle stands high above the valley of the river Churnet, amidst magnificent scenery that has been described as 'the Rhineland of Staffordshire'. It may originally have been built by Bertram de Verdun in the late 12th century: some fragments of masonry of that period survive. The first documentary reference, however, is in 1316, when the male line of the de Verduns died out. The castle passed to the Furnivalle family and from that family, through marriage, to John Talbot, who was created earl of Shrewsbury in 1442. The castle was probably rebuilt in the early 15th century. John, 2nd earl of Shrewsbury, was killed in 1460 at the battle of Northampton, fighting for the Yorkist cause. During the Civil War the castle became a parliamentary garrison and suffered much damage. Charles, 12th earl and 1st and only duke of Shrewsbury, was one of the signatories of the invitation to William of Orange in 1688. In 1714 he again played an important part in national affairs when on the death of Queen Anne he signed the document proclaiming George, the elector of Hanover, as king of England. The Talbot family did not live at Alton until the 19th century. In 1814 Charles, the 15th earl, began to enlarge Alton Lodge, about half a mile to the north of the castle, and to lay out the area between the house and the river in a series of gardens and terraces with architectural follies of Gothic and Chinese character. His nephew and successor John, the 16th earl, continued the work. The house, now called Alton Towers, was further enlarged into a handsome Gothic mansion, in part by A. W. N. Pugin. Today the house is largely a shell, but the gardens have been converted into a popular resort. The castle is occupied by the boys' preparatory school.

The Saxon fortress of Tamworth was granted about 1070 to Robert de Marmion. The earliest Norman defences are earthworks of a motte and bailey type built soon after the Conquest. Later a stone keep and tower were erected. The castle passed in 1294 to the Freville family and from them in 1423 to Sir Thomas Ferrers, son of the 5th Baron Ferrers of Groby. The castle was in ruins at the time of John Leland's visit about 1540. In the 16th and 17th centuries a large house was built within the keep. The Groby and Chartley branches of the Ferrers family were re-united in 1688, when Anne Ferrers, heiress of Tamworth Castle, married Robert Shirley, eldest son of the 1st Baron Ferrers of Chartley. Their daughter and heiress Elizabeth carried the property in marriage to James Compton, 5th earl of Northampton. In 1751 Northampton's daughter and heiress Charlotte married George Townshend of Raynham, Norfolk, who was created Marquess Townshend in 1787. The Townshends retained the castle until 1897, when the 5th marquess sold it to Tamworth corporation. It had been abandoned as a residence in the late 17th century, and from 1790 to 1792 the banqueting hall was used as a forge in connection with the cotton factory of Robert Peel the elder. The castle is now a museum, and the grounds have been converted into gardens and a pleasure park.

*Tamworth castle:*
*the hall*

The Bagots of Blithfield are one of the oldest established families in Staffordshire, as their motto *'Antiquum Obtinens'*—'Possessing Antiquity'—proclaims. Domesday Book records that Bagod held land at Bramshall near Uttoxeter. In 1194 Hervey Bagot, who had married the sister and heiress of his feudal lord, Robert de Stafford, secured the Stafford lands and adopted the Stafford name. This connection between the the two families was one which his 16th-century descendant, Edward, Lord Stafford, was unwilling to acknowledge. In 1590 he wrote to Richard Bagot:

> Like as the High Sheriff of this Shire lately told me that you pretend my name to be Bagot and not Stafford, which untrue speeches you have said unto divers others although some drunken ignorant herald by you corrupted therein hath soothed your lying, I do therefore answer you, that I do better know the descents and matches of my own lineage than any creature can inform me, for in all my records, pedigrees and arms from the first Lord Stafford that was possessed of this castle afore the Conquest bearing the very same coat I now do—the field gold a chevron gules—I cannot find that any Stafford hath married with a Bagot or they with him . . . we have been nine descents barons and earls of Stafford before any Bagot was known in this shire, for Busshe, Bagot and Green were but raised by King Richard the Second . . . No, surely I will not exchange my name of Stafford for the name of a bag of oats, for that is your name, 'Bag Ote'.

Richard Bagot was the representative of the junior branch of the Bagot family which had remained at Bramshall until 1362, when Ralph

Bagot acquired by marriage the manor of Blithfield near Abbots Bromley. His elder son, Sir John Bagot (1358–1437), was a privy councillor to Henry IV and fought with Henry V at Agincourt. His younger son, Sir William Bagot of Baginton in Warwickshire, was a favourite of Richard II, and is believed to be the Bagot of Shakespeare's *Richard II*. Sir John's grandson Richard was killed fighting for Henry Tudor at Bosworth in 1485. Sir Hervey Bagot, the 1st baronet (created in 1627), supported the king's cause in the Civil War; the Blithfield estates were duly confiscated by parliament and were recovered only on payment of a fine of over £1,000. Edward, the 1st baronet's eldest son, did not participate actively in the war, but the two younger sons, Hervey and Richard, both became colonels in the royalist army. Richard was for a time governor of the garrison at Lichfield and was mortally wounded at the battle of Naseby in Northamptonshire in 1645. There is a memorial plaque to him in Lichfield cathedral. For almost 100 years after 1679 the Bagots virtually monopolised one of the two county seats in parliament. As Tories they adopted an attitude of independence towards the Hanoverians, but finally accepted a peerage in 1780. There is evidence that a hall was built at Blithfield in 1398. In the late 16th century Richard Bagot built the present south range with its tall clustered chimneys and steep-pitched gables. There were further alterations in the 18th century, and in the 1820s the 2nd baron employed John Buckler to give the house a romantic neo-Gothic dress, resulting in its present appearance. The house has now been converted into a number of private flats.

The 16th century saw the rise of several new families in the county whose wealth was based on trade. The Levesons of Wolverhampton provide a typical example of this process of social mobility. They had prospered in the wool trade locally and in London, and then established themselves socially by intermarriage with the gentry and the purchase of landed estates. They acquired Trentham priory and other monastic lands soon after the Dissolution. Sir Richard Leveson was the admiral of the English fleet which destroyed the Spanish fleet off Kinsale, Ireland, in December 1601. In the early 1630s Frances, the Leveson co-heiress, married Sir Thomas Gower, Bt., of Stittenham, Yorkshire, who changed his name to Leveson-Gower. The family rose rapidly in the next five generations: they acquired a barony in 1703 and an earldom in 1746, were made marquesses of Stafford in 1786, and became dukes of Sutherland in 1833. The 2nd marquess made the greatest of the family's numerous splendid matches when in 1785 he married Elizabeth, countess of Sutherland and baroness of Strathnaver. He took the title Sutherland as a compliment to his wife when he

*Statue of Admiral Sir Richard Leveson in St Peter's church, Wolverhampton*

39

was created duke in 1833. There is a monument to him overlooking Trentham Park, the Sutherlands' former estate near Newcastle under Lyme. The figure was sculpted by Sir Francis Chantrey in 1836, who also executed a second statue in Trentham church in 1838.

The family seat at Trentham was originally built in the 1630s. The Caroline manor house was replaced by one of Classical style, to the designs of Francis Smith, in the earlier 18th century. Capability Brown and Henry Holland added to the house and landscape between 1768 and 1778. Finally Charles Barry, from 1834 to 1844, rebuilt the hall in an Italianate style. Barry with W. A. Nesfield also laid out the Italian gardens in front of the house. Disraeli described the hall—which he called 'Brentham'—in his novel *Lothair*. The house attracted many distinguished visitors in the 19th century, including the future Edward VII. Meanwhile the pleasant character of Trentham Park was marred by the smell of sewage and effluent which the Potteries towns fed into the river Trent before it passed through the park. It was remarked in 1867 that 'the pools of the princely grounds of Trentham are literally becoming the cesspool of the Potteries'. By 1905 the family had abandoned Trentham as a permanent residence. In 1910 the 4th duke of Sutherland offered the hall to the new county borough of Stoke on Trent. When the offer was refused the duke decided to demolish the building. The sale of the stone and timber took place in September 1911. Part of the west front with its porte-cochère and the stable block survive, and the belvedere tower was erected in the grounds of Sandon Hall by the earl of Harrowby. The princely grounds of Trentham have been developed as a conference, exhibition, and leisure centre.

*Trentham: the mausoleum built for the Leveson-Gower family in 1807-8*

The family of William, 1st Baron Paget, may have originated in Staffordshire. There is a tradition that William's father, John, was born in Wednesbury, but in the early 16th century he was living in London and became a serjeant-at-mace. He prospered sufficiently to send William to Cambridge. Through the influence of Stephen Gardiner, later bishop of Winchester, Paget entered the service of Henry VIII in 1529, and his talents brought him quick promotion. He was knighted in 1537, became principal secretary of state in 1543, and in 1547, on the death of Henry VIII, was made a member of Edward VI's regency council. In 1546 he had acquired the lands of the former Burton abbey and also property in the Cannock Chase area belonging to the bishop of Coventry and Lichfield, including the episcopal residence at Beaudesert. His younger son, Thomas, 3rd Baron Paget, rebuilt Beaudesert Hall in the 1570s. He was a Roman Catholic and was suspected of complicity in the Throckmorton Plot of 1583. He fled to France and was attainted by parliament. His son, William, the 4th baron, was brought up as a Protestant and had his lands restored

40

11. Croxden Abbey: the south transept and the east range of the cloister with the entrance to the chapter house. (*National Monuments Record of the Royal Commission on Historical Monuments, England.*)

Burton Abbey: the church from the south-west. Engraving of 1661 by W. Hollar. (*W. Dugdale*, Monasticon Anglicanum, *ii (1661)*.)

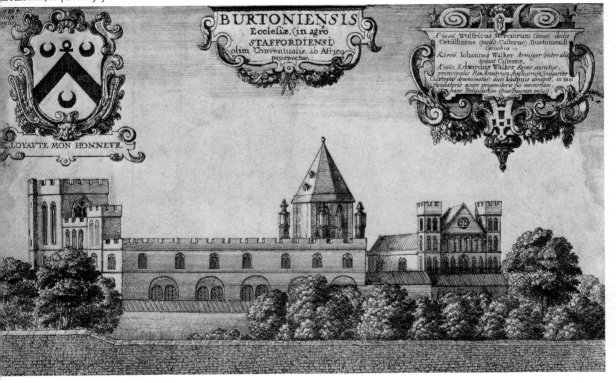

13. Lichfield Cathedral from the south-west in 1961. To the south is Minster Pool; to the east is Stowe Pool, with St Chad's church beyond. (*Aerofilms Ltd.*)

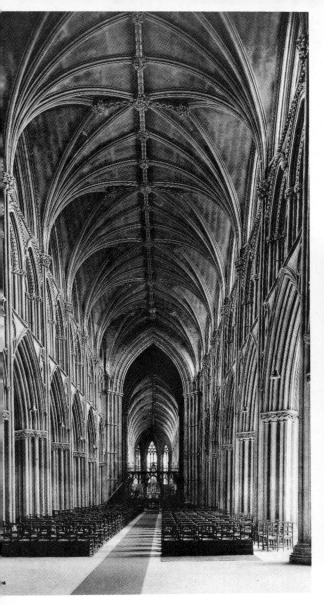

hfield Cathedral

(*above*) the nave looking east.
(*right*) the chapter house.
otographs by H. Felton; National
uments Record.)

16. Brewood church: tombs of Sir Thomas Giffard (d. 1560) and (*behind*) John Giffard (d. 1615). (*Country Life.*)

17. Roman Catholic school at Park Hall, Sedgley, c.1797. Engraving from a drawing by R. Paddey. (*William Salt Lib...*

in 1597 and his title in 1604. William, the 5th baron, fought for the king in the Civil War and his estates were sequestered, but thereafter the family moved up in wealth and title. Henry, the 7th baron, was created earl of Uxbridge in 1714. Henry, the 10th Baron Paget and 2nd earl of Uxbridge, was the duke of Wellington's cavalry commander at the battle of Waterloo in 1815. He had previously run away with Lady Charlotte Wellesley, wife of Wellington's brother, and the divorce proceedings were the sensation of 1809-10. At Waterloo Paget lost a leg, but shortly after received the title of marquess of Anglesey for his services. Much of the Staffordshire property of the 6th marquess was sold in 1919, and the family has lived at Plas Newydd, Anglesey, since 1920. In 1935 Beaudesert Hall, which had been offered to but refused by a number of public bodies, was demolished.

The Sneyds of Keele provide an example of a Staffordshire family which was important and influential but without a title. In the early 15th century they were substantial local landowners with their chief seat at Bradwell, near Newcastle under Lyme. They developed their main interests, however, in Cheshire, and members of the family served as mayors of Chester in 1516-17, 1531-2 and 1543-4. In 1544 William Sneyd bought the manor of Keele, which had earlier belonged to the Knights Templar and then, until the Reformation, to the Hospitallers. About 1580 his son Ralph built what the Staffordshire historian, Sampson Erdeswick, described soon afterwards as 'a very proper and fine house of stone' at Keele. The family actively supported the royalist cause in the Civil War. Colonel Ralph Sneyd was killed in 1651 fighting against the parliamentarians, and the family incurred heavy financial penalties for its loyalty. The Sneyds continued to support the Stuart cause after the revolution of 1688. Ralph Sneyd, a staunch Jacobite, was one of a number of people indicted for rioting in Newcastle under Lyme in 1715, when the Unitarian meeting house was burned down. In the later 18th century the Sneyds developed their coal and iron interests in the locality. They made their peace with the Hanoverians, and Colonel Walter Sneyd commanded King George III's personal bodyguard for 14 years in the late 18th and early 19th centuries. In the 1850s there was a complete rebuilding of Keele Hall in a Jacobean style to the design of Anthony Salvin. The family income diminished in the late 19th century, and Keele Hall was leased to the exiled Grand Duke Michael of Russia from 1901 to 1910. Troops were billeted in the hall during both World Wars. In 1949 the hall and 154 acres were sold to Stoke on Trent corporation, which transferred them to the new University College of North Staffordshire, from 1962 the University of Keele. The university

*The 1st marquess of Anglesey*

41

coat of arms incorporates the Sneyd device, a scythe, and the family's motto 'Thanke God for All'.

The Giffards came to England with the Conqueror in 1066, and the family has held Chillington in Brewood parish from about 1178. Members of other branches of the family occupied high positions of state in medieval England. Some of the Chillington Giffards were knights, and Sir John Giffard held various offices in the household of Henry VIII and was a leading political figure in Staffordshire. It was he who rebuilt the moated house, probably in the 1540s. After the Reformation the family remained firm Catholics, and John Giffard (died 1613) was imprisoned for not conforming to the established Church of England. During the Civil War the family supported Charles I. Chillington Hall became a royalist garrison and was besieged. A document drawn up at the Restoration described Peter Giffard (1581–1663) as a 'great sufferer'. His son Charles had a share in Charles II's escape after the battle of Worcester in 1651, and Boscobel, just over the Shropshire border, where the king hid in an oak tree, belonged to the family. Eventually the family fortunes recovered sufficiently for Peter Giffard, soon after his succession in 1718, to employ Francis Smith of Warwick to rebuild the south wing of the house. Long avenues of oak trees were also planted at this time. Between 1756 and 1776 Thomas Giffard, Peter's grandson, employed Capability Brown and James Paine to landscape the grounds. The village of Chillington was removed in the extension of the park. Finally in the late 1780s John Soane completed the rebuilding of the house for Thomas's son, Thomas. The saloon is thought to occupy the site of the great hall of the former Tudor house, and Soane added the long east front with its pedimented portico.

Another 18th-century house is Shugborough Hall. Before the Reformation the estate belonged to the bishops of Coventry and Lichfield. William Anson of Dunston, a successful lawyer, acquired the property in 1624. His grandson William began about 1693 to build the three-storey block which forms the centre of the present house. Thomas Anson, son of this William, perhaps with the financial assistance of his brother, Admiral George Anson, added flanking pavilions about 1748. When the admiral died in 1762 Thomas inherited his fortune and employed James ('Athenian') Stuart to remove the village of Shugborough and to add a number of Classical monuments to those which had recently been erected. Thomas's great-nephew, who was also called Thomas and was created Viscount Anson in 1806, employed Samuel Wyatt to complete the house. Wyatt also added the portico of eight Ionic columns in 1794. Thomas, 2nd Viscount Anson, was created earl of Lichfield in 1831; he was postmaster-general when the penny post was

*Triumphal arch of the 1760s in the park at Shugborough*

42

introduced. He was addicted to horse racing, and his losses, together with heavy expenditure on electioneering, obliged him to sell the entire contents of Shugborough, except the family portraits, in 1842. On the death of the 4th earl in 1960 Shugborough was offered to the Treasury in lieu of death duties. The Treasury passed it to the National Trust, and the Trust leased it to Staffordshire county council, which established a county museum in the stables. The 5th earl, who occupies part of the house, has established an international reputation as a photographer.

Among the oldest surviving houses is West Bromwich Manor House. This is an example of a moated house, dating from about 1300 and probably built for the Marnham family. Additions, including a chapel, were made to the house in the 15th century. Further improvements were made for the Stanley family in the 16th century, including a kitchen block and a gatehouse, built about 1600. The manor was bought by a Birmingham merchant, Sir Richard Shelton, in 1626. The Shelton family fortunes declined, and in 1720 the house and the estate were sold to Sir Samuel Clarke, a London merchant. He was an enthusiastic horticulturalist who stocked the garden with grapes, nectarines, peaches and figs. The house, after being divided into

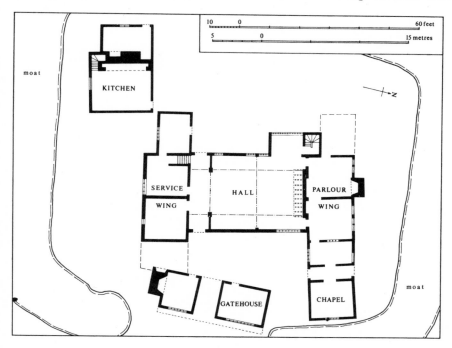

*West Bromwich Manor House*

43

tenements in the 19th century, was in a dilapidated condition by 1950, when it was bought by West Bromwich corporation. It was intended to demolish the house to make way for a small park, but local pressure ensured the preservation of the house, which has been most successfully restored.

*West Bromwich Manor House:*
*the hall*

# VI  Churches and Monasteries

Staffordshire's greatest church is the cathedral at Lichfield. There was probably a church there before St Chad, bishop of the Mercians, 669-72, established his see at Lichfield. The church which he occupied may have been on the site of the later cathedral or to the east at Stowe, where a church dedicated to St Chad and St Chad's Well can still be found. In 700 Bishop Headda built a new church on the site where the cathedral has stood ever since. The saint's relics were transferred from his nearby tomb to a shrine in the new cathedral. Soon afterwards Bede tells of the miracles of healing connected with them and describes the shrine:

> Chad's place of burial is a wooden coffin in the shape of a little house, having an aperture in its side, through which those who visit it out of devotion can insert their hands and take out a little of the dust. When it is put in water and given either to cattle or to men who are ailing, they get their wish and are at once freed from their ailments and rejoice in health restored.

A new shrine was built by Bishop Langton (1296-1321) at a cost of £2,000. The relics attracted many pilgrims and valuable offerings— £400 a year by the 1530s. The shrine was destroyed at the Reformation, but the bones passed into Roman Catholic custody. They eventually found a resting-place in the Roman Catholic cathedral of St Chad at Birmingham, opened in 1841, and there they remain.

The medieval diocese covered Staffordshire, Derbyshire, Cheshire, and parts of Warwickshire, Shropshire and Lancashire. The see was not always at Lichfield. In 1075, as part of the Norman reform of the Church, it was moved from the insignificant Lichfield to the important town of Chester. In 1102 it was moved to Coventry—because, it was said, Bishop Limesey had his eye on the wealth of the monks there. The canons of Lichfield had to struggle hard before Lichfield was again formally recognised as a cathedral in 1228. Even then the diocese was styled Coventry and Lichfield, and the canons of Lichfield had to share the right of electing the bishop with the monks of Coventry. When Coventry priory was dissolved at the Reformation, the Lichfield canons became the only chapter once more, but in 1541 the northern part of the diocese was detached to form the new diocese of Chester. In 1661 the bishop changed his style to Lichfield and Coventry, and in

*St Luke, from the 8th-century Gospels acquired by Lichfield cathedral probably in the 10th century*

45

*Bishop Hacket*

1836, with the transfer of the archdeaconry of Coventry to the see of Worcester, the diocese was again called simply Lichfield. Derbyshire was removed in 1878 so that the diocese thereafter covered only Staffordshire and part of Shropshire.

A rebuilding of Lichfield cathedral was begun by Bishop Limesey (1086–1117), who is said to have used the wealth of the Coventry monks for the purpose. Bishop Peche (1121–6) and Bishop Clinton (1129–48) completed the rebuilding. The cathedral as it stands today dates mainly from the 13th and 14th centuries. It was severely damaged when the Close was besieged during the Civil War, and it was repaired by Bishop Hacket (1661–71), whose work included the rebuilding of the central spire. James Wyatt was called in to carry out repairs in the late 18th century. In 1802 the dean and chapter bought some fine 16th-century glass from the dissolved Cistercian abbey of Herckenrode, near Liège; this, with more glass of the same period acquired in 1894, adorns the 14th-century Lady Chapel at the east end of the cathedral. A restoration lasting nearly 60 years was begun in 1842, much of it the work of George Gilbert Scott, and in recent years more work has been carried out. With its three spires the cathedral has a particularly fine silhouette. The west front with its rows of statues is a late 19th-century attempt to recreate the medieval splendour, described about 1600 by Sampson Erdeswick of Sandon, who wrote the first history of Staffordshire. He considered the west front

> exceedingly finely cut and cunningly set forth with a great number of tabernacles; and in the same, the images or pictures of the prophets, apostles, kings of Judah, and divers other kings of this land, so well embossed and so lively cut that it is a great pleasure for any man, that takes delight to see rarities, to behold them.

The county's varied churches include masterpieces such as the little Norman church of St Chad at Stafford, fine medieval buildings at Brewood and Eccleshall, Christopher Wren's church of 1676 at Ingestre, east of Stafford, and G. F. Bodley's church of the Holy Angels at Hoar Cross built in memory of Hugo Francis Meynell Ingram of Hoar Cross Hall by his widow in 1872–6. There is also the group of collegiate churches at Penkridge, Stafford, Tamworth, Tettenhall, and Wolverhampton, probably originating in the 10th or 11th centuries. Royal in foundation or early patronage, for centuries they enjoyed exemption from the bishop's authority and special royal protection. They were therefore known as royal free chapels. The fine parish church at Gnosall was probably of similar origin, but it did not develop on the same fully collegiate and independent lines as the others.

Exemption from episcopal authority led sometimes to violent quarrels between the canons serving these churches and the bishop.

*Ingestre church*

46

One such case occurred in 1258 when Bishop Meuland came on a visitation of St Mary's at Stafford a month after his consecration as bishop. He seems to have expected trouble, for he brought an armed following. Finding the doors barred against him, he broke his way in, and some of the canons were wounded in the struggle. Nor did independence always lend itself to a high standard of religious life. Peter of Blois, a notable churchman and writer, was dean of St Peter's, Wolverhampton, by 1191. He found standards deplorably low, and after failing in his attempt at reform he resigned in disgust, probably in 1202. He persuaded King John and the archbishop of Canterbury to replace the canons with monks. He also wrote a long letter to the Pope, giving details of the canons' evil ways and urging him to support the change:

*Hoar Cross church*

> While I was piercing the meaning of the Scriptures they would be singing their disgraceful songs . . . They publicly and openly preach fornication like Sodom its own sin, and they took as wives each other's daughters or nieces in the very face of popular infamy . . . Convert this sty of pigs, this hiding-place of Satan, into a temple of God, a dwelling place of the Holy Spirit.

Only the death of the archbishop in 1205 saved the canons.

The canons serving the royal free chapels lived to some extent a common life under a simple rule. They can therefore be seen as part of the re-establishment of monastic life in the county, after the ravages of the Danes had probably put an end to earlier monasteries. The monastic history of Staffordshire starts again in earnest at the beginning of the 11th century with the foundation of the Benedictine abbey at Burton upon Trent by Wulfric Spot, an important landowner in the Midlands. Though not among the great abbeys by national standards, Burton remained the most important of the county's religious houses. With an annual income of over £39 in 1086 and nearly £514 in 1535, it was by far the richest; with its 31 professed monks in 1295 and 22 in 1524 it also had the largest recorded community. Its Annals are a major source for the political history of England in the 13th century, largely perhaps because the abbey's position at an important crossing of the Trent brought a continual stream of visitors. These included several kings from William the Conqueror onwards, and one of the rooms in the abbey came to be called the King's Chamber. The abbey's situation brought it into national politics in 1322 during the rebellion of Thomas, earl of Lancaster, against Edward II. The earl occupied Burton bridge in an unsuccessful attempt to stop the royal troops from crossing the Trent, and meantime he stored his treasure in the abbey. Before retreating, he set fire to the town, and the abbey evidently suffered at the

47

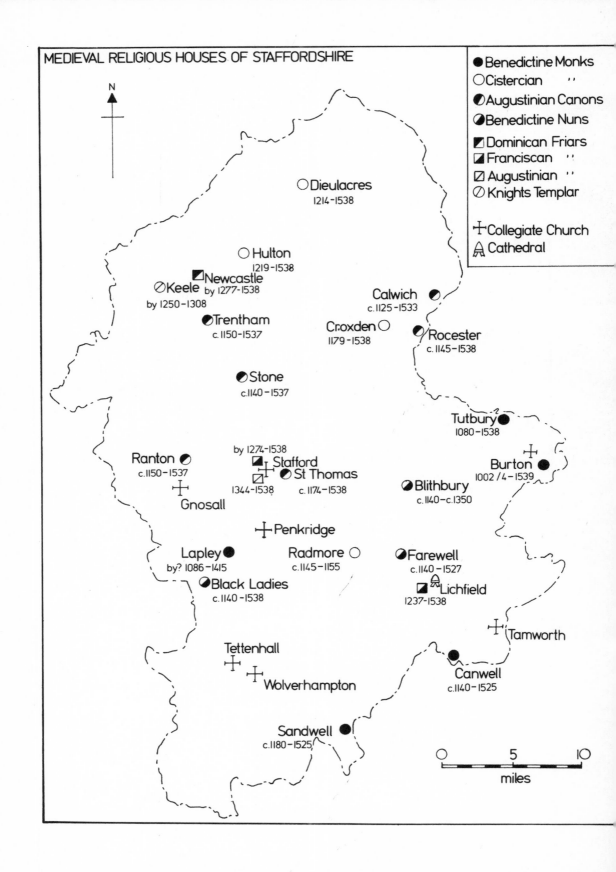

MEDIEVAL RELIGIOUS HOUSES OF STAFFORDSHIRE

**Legend:**
- ● Benedictine Monks
- ○ Cistercian "
- ◐ Augustinian Canons
- ◑ Benedictine Nuns
- ◨ Dominican Friars
- ◧ Franciscan "
- ▨ Augustinian "
- ⊘ Knights Templar
- ☩ Collegiate Church
- ⛪ Cathedral

○ Dieulacres
1214-1538

○ Hulton
1219-1538

◨ Newcastle
by 1277-1538

⊘ Keele
by 1250-1308

● Calwich
c.1125-1533

◐ Trentham
c.1150-1537

Croxden ○
1179-1538

◐ Rocester
c.1145-1538

◐ Stone
c.1140-1537

Tutbury ●
1080-1538

Ranton ◐
c.1150-1537

by 1274-1538

◨ Stafford
▨ ◐ St Thomas
1344-1538   c.1174-1538

Burton ●
1002/4-1539

☩ Gnosall

◑ Blithbury
c.1140-c.1350

☩ Penkridge

Lapley ●
by? 1086-1415

Radmore ○
c.1145-1155

◐ Farewell
c.1140-1527

◑ Black Ladies
c.1140-1538

◧ ⛪ Lichfield
1237-1538

☩ Tamworth

Tettenhall
☩

☩ Wolverhampton

● Canwell
c.1140-1525

Sandwell ●
c.1180-1525

○ 5    10
miles

18.   Josiah Wedgwood and his family in the grounds of Etruria Hall in 1780. Painting by George Stubbs.(*The Wedgwood Museum, Barlaston, Stoke on Trent.*)

19.   Caverswall Castle from the south-west when occupied by Benedictine nuns. Aquatint published in 1817. (*William Salt Library.*)

Queen Street Congregational church, Wolverhampton. (*Wolverhampton Central Library.*)
20. (*above*) the building of 1813.
21. (*below*) the building of 1866.

22. The opening of the Sikh temple in the former Congregational church at Smethwick in 1961. On the speaker's right are P.C. Gordon-Walker, then M.P. for Smethwick, and the mayor and mayoress of Smethwick. (*Birmingham Evening Mail.*)

*So I am to take back the Old Shoes — well I thought you would never desert the old Staffordshire shop, — well it is very wonderfull! — after being a Customer so many Years, and more over when we gave you such Credit. I was a going to say, when no one else would trust you!!*

*Why my good friend only observe how neat this Westminster cut is, what fine upper leathers, — but however the Old Shoes are in good condition yet so you may give them to Tom. — for you know I do not like a good thing to go out of the Family!!*

NEW SHOES or a Visit from a Staffordshire Elector.

Pub.<sup>d</sup> Nov.<sup>r</sup> 1806 by Walker, N.<sup>o</sup> 7 Cornhill.

23. A cartoon of 1806 showing Richard Brinsley Sheridan abandoning his parliamentary seat at Stafford. (*William Salt Library.*)

24. Wolverhampton racecourse at the time of its establishment in 1825. The town is shown in the background witl
Peter's church on the left and St John's (1755-60) on the right. Based on a drawing by R. Noyes. (*William Salt Libr*

25. Bradley ironworks near Bilston in 1836. Watercolour drawing by R. Noyes. (*William Salt Library.*)

rebels' hands. The abbot was later accused of having retained the earl's treasure and had some difficulty in clearing himself.

The next foundation after Burton may have been the small Benedictine priory at Lapley, west of Stafford, a dependency of the abbey of St Remigius at Rheims. In 1061 the monks of Rheims gave burial to Burchard, son of Alfgar, earl of Mercia, who died there on his way back from Rome. In fulfilment of his son's dying promise Alfgar gave the monks land at Lapley and elsewhere in Staffordshire. They duly established a cell at Lapley, possibly within 25 years of the gift. The only other Staffordshire foundation of the time was the Benedictine priory of Tutbury, founded in 1080 by Henry de Ferrers close to his castle.

The 12th century was the great period of monastic foundations in the county. The nobility and gentry were the main patrons, but royalty was responsible for bringing the Cistercians into the county. That order, which aimed at recovering a primitive austerity, favoured remote sites, and its first Staffordshire house was at Radmore in the heart of Cannock forest. It was originally a hermitage, endowed by King Stephen in the later 1130s, but the Empress Maud, Stephen's rival for the English throne and a supporter of the Cistercians, persuaded the hermits to adopt the Cistercian rule about 1145. The abbey was short lived, for the monks found the royal foresters a great nuisance, and they approached Maud's son, Henry II, on his coronation day in December 1154 for help. He gave them land at Stoneleigh in Warwickshire in exchange for Radmore. The monks arrived at Stoneleigh the following June, and Henry turned Radmore into a hunting lodge. Later Cistercian houses in the county were all in the remote moorlands of the north-east. Another order which benefited from royal patronage was that of the Knights Templar. Henry II gave them an estate at Keele in the late 1160s, and they established a preceptory there, evidently by the 1250s.

The earls of Chester and their family were notable patrons. The Benedictine priory at Canwell on the county boundary south-west of Tamworth was founded about 1140 by Geva, illegitimate daughter of Hugh, earl of Chester. Ranulph de Gernon, the turbulent earl of Chester of Stephen's reign, founded the house of Augustinian canons at Trentham, possibly on his deathbed in 1153. His grandson, Ranulph de Blundeville, was the founder of the Cistercian abbey of Dieulacres, near Leek, in 1214. The abbey chronicle relates how the younger Ranulph was visited in a dream by his grandfather, who instructed him to transfer the Cistercians of Poulton in Cheshire to the new site; Poulton had been founded by Ranulph the grandfather and was suffering at the hands of the Welsh. Ranulph the grandson told his wife about his

*Seal of Rocester abbey in use in 1490*

49

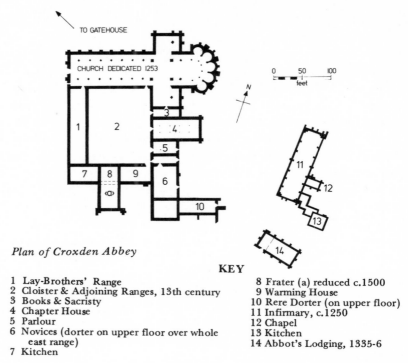

TO GATEHOUSE

CHURCH DEDICATED 1253

N

0  50  100
feet

*Plan of Croxden Abbey*

**KEY**

1 Lay-Brothers' Range
2 Cloister & Adjoining Ranges, 13th century
3 Books & Sacristy
4 Chapter House
5 Parlour
6 Novices (dorter on upper floor over whole east range)
7 Kitchen

8 Frater (a) reduced c.1500
9 Warming House
10 Rere Dorter (on upper floor)
11 Infirmary, c.1250
12 Chapel
13 Kitchen
14 Abbot's Lodging, 1335-6

dream and the proposed new abbey. She, a Frenchwoman, exclaimed 'Deuxencres' (May God grant it increase). Thus the abbey came to be called Dieulacres.

Some of the bishops of the diocese were also patrons of the religious. Bishop Clinton (1129–48) founded the Benedictine nunnery at Farewell, near Lichfield, and probably also that at Brewood; he was also a benefactor of the Cistercians at Radmore. Bishop Peche helped to found the Augustinian priory near Stafford dedicated to St Thomas Becket within a few years of the saint's murder in Canterbury cathedral in 1170. In 1182 Bishop Peche resigned his see and became a canon at the new priory; he died there later the same year. Bishop Stavensby brought the Franciscan friars to Lichfield, probably in 1237.

The last religious house to be founded in the county was the Augustinian friary at Forebridge, Stafford, established in 1344 by Ralph, Lord Stafford. During the Hundred Years' War with France (which started in 1337), Tutbury and Lapley suffered as dependencies of French mother houses. Tutbury survived, but Lapley was suppressed, its possessions being granted by the Crown in 1415 to the new college at Tong in Shropshire. In the 1520s Cardinal Wolsey suppressed several small houses. In Staffordshire the decayed Benedictine priories of Canwell and of Sandwell in West Bromwich were dissolved in 1525 and their endowments given to the cardinal's new college at Oxford,

50

the present Christ Church; the few monks were transferred to other houses. In the same way Wolsey suppressed the nunnery at Farewell in 1527; on that occasion the property was given to the choristers of Lichfield cathedral.

The way was thus prepared for Henry VIII's attack in the 1530s. The first Staffordshire house to go was the little Augustinian priory of Calwich in the north-east. The death of the prior in 1530 left only one canon there. In 1532 the Crown and the patron, Sir Ralph Longford, made an agreement for the suppression of the priory, and the process was completed the following year. The Crown seized the property, sold the goods, and leased the site to Longford. Many of the smaller houses were suppressed under an Act of Parliament in 1536, and from 1538 the rest surrendered—'voluntarily', according to the fiction of the time. The last Staffordshire house to go was the oldest, Burton abbey; it surrendered on 14 November 1539. In 1541 it was re-established by the king as a college of canons, but that foundation was short lived, being suppressed in 1545 under an Act of that year. The rest of the colleges in the county were dissolved in 1548 under an Act of 1547. That was the end of the royal free chapels, except for Wolverhampton, which was restored by Mary I in 1553. It survived until 1848 when it fell victim to a new age of reform.

*Croxden abbey: the west front*

All the possessions of the religious orders passed to the Crown, which soon sold most of them. The nobility and gentry, once the patrons of the orders, now became involved in a scramble for the monastic property. Thus in 1536 and 1537 counter-bids were made for the Augustinian priory at Ranton, near Stafford, by George Blount, by Sir Simon Harcourt (the descendant of the founder), and by Henry, Lord Stafford, who pleaded his 12 children and his poverty; the Harcourts eventually won. Rowland Lee, bishop of Coventry and Lichfield, requested St Thomas's priory on behalf of 'the poor boys, my nephews'; he was successful, but it is ironical that Brian Fowler, the nephew who settled at St Thomas's, established an important Roman Catholic centre there. The religious themselves were granted pensions by the Crown, but payment was not always forthcoming. The abbot of Dieulacres received a pension of £60, and the remaining 12 monks pensions varying from £6 to £2; but in December 1540 the ex-abbot was writing to one of the royal officials begging for the payments due to himself and his 'poor brethren'.

A few of the monastic churches remained parish churches after the Dissolution, as at Stone and Trentham. Otherwise the buildings quickly fell into ruin, and little now survives. The ruins of the Cistercian abbey at Croxden in the north-east, founded in the 1170s by Bertram de Verdun, lord of Alton, are the most extensive. The buildings were

51

usually quarried for their stone or left to fall after the lead and other fittings had been removed. At Calwich the Fleetwoods, who secured the site in 1544, made the church into a house, turning the chancel into a parlour, the nave into a hall, and the tower into a kitchen.

The priests serving the Roman Catholics of England after the Reformation included some members of religious orders, but they were usually isolated individuals. The Stafford family of Stafford Castle and the Colemans of Cannock each had a Benedictine monk as a chaplain in the early 17th century. The new order of the Jesuits became established in the county about 1613, probably under the wing of the Roman Catholic Biddulph family of Biddulph in the north of the county. From the later 17th century the Franciscan friars, working from over the Warwickshire boundary, first from Birmingham and then from Edgbaston, served Roman Catholics in the adjoining Handsworth and Harborne, then still part of Staffordshire.

With the Roman Catholic revival from the late 18th century onwards new religious houses were established. The first in Staffordshire was at Caverswall Castle, east of the Potteries. There, under the wing of the Coyney family, Benedictine nuns from Ghent, who had fled to England with the advance of the French Revolution, opened a convent in 1811. The first English house belonging to the Congregation of the Oratory, predecessor of the present Oratories at Edgbaston in Birmingham, and Brompton in London, was opened at Cotton in north-east Staffordshire with John Henry Newman, the future cardinal, as superior. Among the many religious communities now working in the county, the Dominican nuns at Stone were established in 1853 by Mother Margaret Hallahan; she moved there from the Foley, between Fenton and Longton, where she had established a community two years before. The sisters now run two schools and a home for invalid ladies. The home for the elderly at Cobridge in the Potteries, run by the Little Sisters of the Poor, was opened in 1892, when the nuns moved there after two years working in Hanley. The Dominican friars at Hawkesyard, near Rugeley, were given the property by Josiah Spode in 1894 and now use it as a conference centre.

*Mother Margaret Hallahan*

# VII Reformers and Recusants

The English Reformation began moderately under Henry VIII, became extreme under Edward VI, suffered a reaction under Mary I, and settled down to the Anglican compromise under Elizabeth I. The process was typified by the attitude of the bishops of Coventry and Lichfield. Rowland Lee (1534–43) was a prominent royal servant who may have officiated at the marriage of Henry VIII and Anne Boleyn in 1533, the year before he got his bishopric. Richard Sampson (1543–54), another civil servant who had been bishop of Chichester since 1536, was able to accommodate himself to both Edward VI and Mary I. Ralph Baynes (1554–9) was a zealous anti-Protestant, and seven heretics were burnt in the diocese during his time, three of them at Lichfield. Like several of his higher clergy he refused to conform to the Elizabethan Settlement and was duly deprived. Opposition to the official religious policy was now beginning.

The first Elizabeth bishop, Thomas Bentham (1559–79), found his diocese recalcitrant, with Staffordshire the most troublesome part of it. The majority of the parish clergy conformed in 1559, but Bentham was soon being criticised for 'disorders used of my clergy'. He duly gave instructions for a visitation of the diocese in 1565, stressing the need for use of the Book of Common Prayer, preaching, clear recitation of the service, and a proper standard of clerical life. Altars were to be replaced by tables, and the churches cleared of 'all monuments of idolatry and superstition as holy water stocks, sepulchres which were used on Good Friday, hand bells, and all manner of idols which be laid up in secret places in your church where Latin service was used'.

Many of the laity, too, were hostile to the new ways, absenting themselves from church and persisting in the use of rosaries and prayers for the dead. There, also, Bentham ordered his clergy to tighten discipline. In 1564 he reported to the government on the religious sympathies of 17 Staffordshire J.P.s, pointing out that no fewer than 10 were 'adversaries of religion'. Other government agents found in 1562 that large numbers of people in Staffordshire 'are generally evil inclined towards religion and forbear coming to church and participating of the sacraments, using also very broad speeches in alehouses and elsewhere'. Immediately after her progress through Staffordshire in 1575, Elizabeth had nine Catholic gentry summoned before the Privy Council, including John Giffard, who had entertained her at Chillington.

*Chillington Hall: the mid-16th century house as shown on an 18th-century estate map*

53

In 1586 Elizabeth moved Mary Queen of Scots from Chartley to Northamptonshire after being repeatedly warned of 'the backwardness' of Staffordshire. At the same time Philip II of Spain was assured that in Staffordshire 'the gentry and common people are strong Catholics and all devoted to the Queen of Scotland'.

The strength of Roman Catholicism in the county stemmed largely from the Catholic sympathies of many of the local nobility and gentry who maintained a Catholic tenantry and provided centres in their houses where Mass could be said by a resident chaplain or an itinerant priest. Such recusancy—the official term for refusal to conform to the Anglican compromise—was maintained in the face of increasingly heavy penalties, from fines to imprisonment and death.

*Bonaventure Giffard, first vicar apostolic of the Midland District*

At first Catholics were dependent on priests who had been deprived by the government for their refusal to conform. As late as 1586 one such priest, John Bradbury, was serving in the household of Dorothy Heveningham at Aston, near Stone. From 1574 there came a new wave of priests who had gone abroad to be trained for priesthood, and returned to minister to their Catholic countrymen in the teeth of the law. An example of their activity in Staffordshire is provided in a letter written in 1582 by one of them, Dr. Henshawe, who relates how he had spent two months in the county with two Jesuits and converted 228 people. In 1620 details were given of the disguises worn by priests visiting Bilston, a place 'much infected with popery and infested with popish priests'. One wore 'a greenish suit, his doublet opened under the armpits with ribbons', and another 'a kind of russet-coloured suit, with a sword by his side. An early martyr was Robert Sutton, born in 1544, the son of a Burton carpenter. He was ordained in the Anglican Church but resigned and went to study in the Low Countries. In 1578 he was ordained a Catholic priest, and returned to England. He was executed at Stafford in 1588, after being caught saying Mass in the house of Erasmus Wolseley in the town. All those present at his Mass were condemned to death, but as a result of popular clamour the laymen were let off with a fine. A local sympathiser described Sutton's end:

> The priest was a very reverend learned man, and at his arraignment disputed very stoutly and learnedly. He only was executed, that was hanged and quartered. And it was done in a most villainous, butcherly manor by one Moseley who with his axe cut off his head (while he had yet sense and was ready to stand up) through the mouth.

A typical Catholic centre was St Thomas, near Stafford, the home of the Fowler family who, having acquired the former Augustinian priory in 1543, maintained a chapel there for nearly 200 years. Bishop Bentham complained in 1564 that Brian Fowler was harbouring the Catholic ex-bishop of Peterborough at St Thomas and that as a result 'divers lewd priests have resort thither'. From 1703 to 1716 another Catholic bishop found a home there, Dr. George Witham, who was the Catholic bishop (officially styled vicar apostolic) for the Midlands. The house was also the home of priests serving as chaplains to the Fowlers; the memorials of two of them, erected in the early 18th century by William Fowler, can still be seen in the nearby Anglican church at Baswich, where they lie buried, a symbol of the influence of the local squire even when a Catholic. In the 1730s St Thomas passed into Protestant hands, and on 29 August 1739 the vicar of Baswich recorded that he had that day performed 'the first baptism from St Thomas since the Reformation'.

The Giffards of Chillington in Brewood parish were similarly influential in the south of the county. The head of the family remained a Catholic until 1861, and until the earlier 19th century most of the tenants on the Chillington estate were Catholics. Brewood Anglican church contains further evidence of the squire's influence in the fine alabaster tombs of Elizabethan and Jacobean Giffards which occupy pride of place in the chancel. The Giffards maintained chapels on their estate. The first vicar apostolic for the Midlands, appointed in 1668, was Bonaventure Giffard, a member of the Wolverhampton branch of the family. From 1756 until 1804 the Giffards gave the vicars apostolic a home at Longbirch on the Chillington estate; one of them is buried in Brewood Anglican church.

It was partly Giffard influence that made Wolverhampton the strongest Catholic centre in the county. There, according to the local Puritan preacher in 1624, 'Rome's snaky brood roosted and rested themselves more warmer and safer and with greater countenance . . . than in any other part of the kingdom'. In the mid–17th century there so many Catholics of all social classes that the town was known as Little Rome. Under the Catholic James II it had a flourishing Jesuit centre. By 1688 six Jesuits were living in the Deanery House in Horse Fair (now Wulfruna Street) and maintained a much-frequented chapel there, and a school attended by nearly 50 local boys. The centre did not survive the Revolution of 1688; the fittings were largely pillaged by the mob or seized by the authorities, and most of the well-stocked library was burnt in the market place. Some 40 years later a new chapel and house were built, much of the cost being met by the Giffards. Now known as Giffard House, it survives as the presbytery of the adjoining church of St Peter and St Paul, built in 1825–7. Caution, however, was long felt to be necessary. In 1754 the Catholics of the town were eager to contribute to the building fund of the new Anglican church of St John because they depended on their Protestant neighbours for trade and also because 'if troublesome times should come

*Longbirch in 1838*

55

again 'twill keep the mob from molesting our chapel, breaking the windows etc.'.

In 1767 and 1780 returns made to the House of Lords of the number of Catholics in the diocese of Lichfield and Coventry showed some 3,000 in Staffordshire, far more than in any other part of the diocese. The return of 1767 is particularly informative. Wolverhampton still led the way with 491, perhaps about a quarter of the town's population. Other areas in the south of the county with large numbers of Catholics were Brewood with 389, a reflection of the Giffards' continuing influence, Sedgley with 253, Handsworth with 132, Bushbury with 117, and Walsall with 110. The Sedgley figure was inflated by a school at Park Hall with 97 boys, a head and five assistant masters; opened in 1763 and attracting boys from all over England, the school moved in 1873 to Cotton in north-east Staffordshire where it remains. In 1767 there were several centres of Catholic population in the north of the county, notably Draycott in the Moors (156), Stone (132), and Swynnerton (100), all examples of gentry protection.

*Roman Catholic church of Holy Trinity, Newcastle under Lyme*

The later 18th century brought growing toleration, culminating in the Act of 1791 which made Catholic chapels legal provided they were registered with the authorities; in Staffordshire 13 were promptly registered. An example of toleration in the south of the county was the wedding of the Catholic Thomas Whitgreave in 1780. He was married in his house at Saredon on 21 June with the Catholic chaplain from Moseley officiating. On 22 June, to comply with the law, the bride, groom, chaplain and guests went to Bushbury parish church where the Anglican curate performed a second ceremony. He then accompanied the party back to Saredon for dinner, and afterwards the chaplain, the curate and the groom's father left for home together.

The Catholics of England were moving into what John Henry Newman hailed in 1852 as their 'Second Spring', with the Catholic Emancipation Act of 1829 as a milestone on the way. Emigré priests fleeing from the French revolution added to the supply of clergy from the 1790s, and several worked in Staffordshire. The first to settle in the county was Louis Martin de Laistre. He came to Mucklestone in north-west Staffordshire about 1794 as tutor to the Anglican rector's children, and for a time he said Mass in the house of a Catholic farmer at Napley Heath. In 1796 he took charge of the Catholic mission at nearby Ashley. Irish immigrants swelled the Catholic population of Staffordshire by the 1820s. By 1851 the 13 chapels of 1791 had increased to 33, with a Catholic population of perhaps some 25,000. By 1884 there were 51 churches and chapels, and the Catholic population was given as 33,643. When Catholic dioceses were established in 1850, Staffordshire was included in the diocese of Birmingham, an archdiocese from 1911.

Growing numbers brought new problems because of the poverty of so many. At Cobridge in the Potteries the increase in numbers meant that the chapel of 1781 had to be extended in 1816, and a school built in 1821; yet in 1834 the priest's weekly income was only twelve shillings. At Walsall in 1851 half the 700 people who heard Mass on Sunday attended a service at 8 a.m. which was described by the priest as 'for poor people who from want of proper clothes do not like to appear out of doors at a later period of the day'. All the same there was a general feeling of optimism by then, symbolised by the church of St Giles at Cheadle, opened in 1846. It was designed by A. W. N. Pugin and paid for by John, earl of Shrewsbury. The interior is richly painted and tiled, and the spire rises triumphantly to 200 feet.

*Roman Catholic church of St Giles, Cheadle*

The Church of England had to face opposition not only from Roman Catholics, but also from Protestants wanting a more thoroughgoing reform than the Elizabethan Settlement provided. By the early 17th century, Protestant dissent had spread through much of Staffordshire. It was strong in Burton upon Trent where a Puritan 'exercise' was held in the 1590s and in the early years of the 17th century. From Burton too came Edward Wightman, the last heretic to be burned at the stake in England. He suffered for his unorthodox views, which included some Baptist opinions, at Lichfield on 11 April 1612. The Puritan vicar of Sedgley, William Fenner, was deprived of his living in 1627, even though he urged his fellow Puritans to remain within the Church of England. Wolverhampton was not only a centre of Roman Catholicism, but also had a strong dissenting element. One well-known dissenter was William Pinson, an attorney, who lived there from 1631 to 1636. He was accused of maintaining conventicles, making extempore prayers, preaching sermons, and expounding the Scriptures.

The Civil War and Commonwealth period gave a stimulus to dissent. Presbyterian opinion was strong among the Staffordshire clergy in 1648, when 36 ministers and two schoolmasters signed the *Testimony*, a militant Presbyterian declaration against the principle of religious toleration. Baptists were active in the north-east in 1644, and they increased in strength in the following years. By the early 1650s they had a large congregation at Stafford which included the military governor, Colonel Henry Danvers. George Fox, the founder of Quakerism, first visited the county in 1651 after being released from Derby gaol. He preached near Burton and went on to Lichfield. In his *Journal* he described how there he had a vision of blood flowing through the streets and went up and down crying 'Woe to the bloody city of Lichfield'. Soon afterwards he preached at Cauldon in the

Moorlands. During the next few years Quakerism spread throughout the county, becoming especially strong in the Moorlands.

Persecution of dissenters began in earnest after 1660 with the penal legislation of the Clarendon Code. The Anglican Church was purged of ministers with Puritan opinions, and it is estimated that nearly half the parish clergy of Staffordshire were evicted from their livings. Known dissenters were brought before the ecclesiastical courts; at Bishop Hacket's visitation of 1668 there were 199 presentations of offenders, of whom 111 were excommunicated. One was Moses Bennett of West Bromwich, accused of 'sitting in church with his hat on and refusing to come to church in time of divine service, saying that he would not come whilst the minister has the devil's clothing, meaning the surplice'. Despite persecution nonconformity persisted. When in 1669 Archbishop Sheldon, himself a Staffordshire man from Stanton, near Ellastone, called for a national report on the number of conventicles, 24 towns and villages in Staffordshire were named.

*The Quaker meeting house, Stafford*

In 1672 Charles II issued his Declaration of Indulgence which suspended the penal laws against Protestant nonconformists and papists, and for Protestants also permitted authorised places of worship and licensed teachers. Before the Declaration was withdrawn in March 1673 licences for 68 houses had been issued in Staffordshire (47 of them Presbyterian) and for 21 teachers (16 Presbyterian). In the so-called Compton Census of 1676 purporting to give the numbers of Anglicans, papists and dissenters, Stafford is shown with 155 nonconformists, and then comes Ipstones with 73 and Grindon with 43, both of them in the north-east. In practice there was a good deal of unofficial toleration even before the Toleration Act of 1689.

Under that Act Protestant dissenters, but not Unitarians, and not Roman Catholics, were relieved of the penalties which they had incurred hitherto by worshipping at unauthorised meetings, provided that they now registered their meeting houses with the authorities. The first registrations in the county were of four houses in Newcastle under Lyme in 1689. Between 1689 and 1750 there were 95 registrations in the county as a whole, 97 from 1750 to 1800, and 874 from 1800 to 1850. Popular feeling against dissenters was still easily aroused in the early 18th century. In 1715, after the failure of the Old Pretender's rebellion, there were widespread riots throughout the Midlands, and particularly in Staffordshire. Meeting houses all over the county were wrecked or damaged, and the government paid £1,723 in compensation.

John Wesley, the founder of Methodism, paid his first visit to Staffordshire in 1738 and his last in 1790. On his earlier visits he was often in danger, as at Wednesbury in 1743 when the mob threatened to 'knock his brains out'. Methodism soon flourished, especially in the growing industrial areas. The first chapel in Staffordshire was built at Tipton in 1755, and the first in the Potteries at Burslem in 1766. On 30 March 1784 Wesley wrote in his *Journal*:

> I preached in the new meeting house at Hanley Green; but this was far too small to hold the congregation. Indeed this country is all on fire, and the flame is still spreading from village to village.

There were five Wesleyan chapels in the Potteries by 1801 and 46 by 1851, while by 1818 the Wednesbury circuit alone had 840 members and 14 preaching places. Most of the converts were people of small means, and the upper classes were generally indifferent or opposed to Wesley. One exception was the 2nd earl of Dartmouth, of Sandwell in West Bromwich, who was Secretary of State for the Colonies from 1772 to 1775. He attended the services at Wednesbury chapel and allowed himself to be addressed there as 'Brother Dartmouth'.

Methodist success was followed by a revival of the older nonconformist sects. Captain Jonathan Scott brought Congregationalism to Newcastle, where he began open-air preaching in 1776. So successful was he that Wesley complained in his *Journal* on 26 March 1781 that the Congregationalists were getting the benefit of his own labours. The movement spread, and there were 19 Congregational chapels in the county by 1800, and 46 by 1850.

In the late 18th and early 19th centuries the Methodist movement split into a number of sects. A group led by Alexander Kilham became dissatisfied with the official Methodist policy of avoiding a clash with the Church of England; they also desired more lay participation in the movement. They broke away and formed the Methodist New Connexion in 1797. One of the leading figures of the sect in the Potteries was Job Ridgway, a pottery manufacturer of Hanley. He and his family played a major part in the history of Bethesda, the first New Connexion chapel in the Potteries, opened at Hanley in 1798. Another offshoot, Primitive Methodism, had working-class origins. It may be said to have been born on Mow Cop, a hill on the Staffordshire-Cheshire boundary north of the Potteries. Two Methodists, Hugh Bourne, a carpenter, and William Clowes, a potter, organised open-air meetings on the hill at which great fervour was displayed. The Methodist Conference disapproved, and Bourne and Clowes were expelled in 1807. They and their followers continued to meet, and in 1811 adopted the name Primitive Methodist. The movement eventually spread through the whole country.

*Hugh Bourne*

The census of religious attendance of 1851 revealed the progress made by nonconformity. In 1851 the county had a total population of 608,716. The census, taken on Sunday, 30 March, showed that

129,962 people attended public worship in the morning, 83,404 in the afternoon, and 83,881 in the evening, a total of 297,247 attendances. Of these, about 46 per cent. were at the Church of England's services, but over 48 per cent. were at Protestant nonconformist places of worship, with Methodists by far the most numerous. Roman Catholics represented 5½ per cent. of worshippers. The 20th century has seen both declining nonconformist numbers and also the appearance of new denominations. Pentecostal churches have increased, catering largely for the West Indian immigrants who have settled in the towns since the Second World War.

Non-Christian religions have increasingly found a place in the county. There was a Jewish synagogue in Hanley from the 1870s, and the Jewish burial ground on the Stone road south of Newcastle was in use by the end of the 19th century. The immigration of the later 20th century has resulted in the opening of temples and mosques, particularly in the south of the county. At Smethwick Sikhs were holding services from the 1950s; in 1961 they bought the Congregational church in High Street dating from the 1850s and re-opened it as the Guru Nanak Gurdwara. In Walsall the Sikhs had a temple by 1964 and rebuilt it in the early 1970s; a second temple was opened in a former Primitive Methodist church in the mid 1960s. Mosques, too, were opened in Walsall from the 1960s. In West Bromwich Ebenezer Congregational church, after being closed in 1971, was converted into the Hindu Shree Krishna temple, with the official opening and installation of idols taking place in 1974.

*The Methodist church of 1864 in Chapel Street, Stafford*

# VIII Royalists and Roundheads

There was some discontent in Staffordshire at the policies of James I and Charles I. Anthony Dyott, M.P. for Lichfield from 1601 to 1614, said in the House of Commons debate of 22 November 1610 that he would vote for the proposed taxes if the king could be restrained from 'imposing', that is, levying extra import duties. In 1616 Sir Walter Bagot, owner of a glassworks in Bagot's Wood near Abbots Bromley, complained of the effects of the glass monopoly on his business. The heavy taxation of the period was sometimes resented. Thus at Walsall in 1636 the mayor and burgesses protested against the levying of ship money.

*Edward Leigh*

When the war broke out on 22 August 1642, however, there was no rush to take sides. A few enthusiasts began to gather troops, but as late as 15 November the sheriff called a meeting at Stafford to attempt to keep the county quiet. He declared that 'riots and unlawful assemblies have been made and committed by certain persons in arrays and warlike manner', and it was agreed that forces should be raised to deal with such disturbances. The officers appointed included both future royalists and parliamentarians. Even after the issue was properly joined many men remained neutral until and unless they were forced to support one side or the other. Religion was a factor in influencing some in their choice. Edward Leigh of Rushall, a man of strong Presbyterian opinions, became an active parliamentarian. Roman Catholics were inclined to support the king rather than parliament. Members of some Catholic families, for example the Lanes of Bentley and the Giffards of Chillington, joined the royal army. Motives other than religion are not readily apparent in the county. Lord Paget of Beaudesert started as a parliamentarian, but later changed to the king 'out of conscience', as he explained in a letter to the House of Lords, and at his own expense raised a regiment that fought at Edgehill in 1642. His fellow peers in Staffordshire were also royalist, with the notable exception of the earl of Essex, the parliamentary commander-in-chief. Of the Protestant gentry in the county only about a dozen became active royalists compared with the 40 or so who were opposed to the king. Men from the commercial elements in the community, like Thomas Backhouse, ironmonger and millmaster of Stafford, are found on the committee which administered the county on parliament's behalf, but economic interests did not obviously prompt more in one direction than in another.

*Robert Devereux, earl of Essex*

In the Moorlands there was genuine popular support among the common people for the parliamentary cause. In February 1643 a body of Moorlanders, led by a person of humble quality known as 'the Grand Juryman' and armed with birding guns, clubs and scythes, marched on Stafford. They were unsuccessful in their aim of ejecting the royalist garrison there, but later in the war, after some training by officers sent by parliament, they were able to play a useful role in some actions. Most of the commoners who joined the royalist or parliamentary forces, however, were influenced to do so by the local magnates or gentry. Many of the recruits to Paget's regiment came from his own estates on Cannock Chase; Walter Kinnersley of Loxley, near Uttoxeter, took four local men with him into the ranks of the parliamentary army. Such recruits were loyal to their individual commanders rather than to the cause which they served, and this was a weakness on both sides, though more apparent among the royalists.

The financial burdens imposed on the civilian population were often heavy. Thus the inhabitants of Hatherton near Cannock paid many levies to the royal forces during the war. An entry in their 'Lewn Book' for 5 June 1643 reads: 'for provisions of oats, butter, cheese for quartering, sent to Pillington Hall, £2'. Where the military control of an area was disputed or changed hands the inhabitants sometimes paid to both sides. The constable's accounts for Mavesyn Ridware for 1643–4 show payments to the royalists at Lichfield of £109 18s. 0d. and to the parliamentary authorities of Stafford of £141 3s. 10d. Trade also was affected. Sir Simon Degge, the Staffordshire antiquary, wrote of Burton upon Trent that 'it was before the last wars a town much given to clothing, their kersies being in great esteem in this country; but since the war it hath declined in trade, having suffered much by the plunder'. Non-combatants in areas of fighting and along the line of march of large armies suffered from the depredations of both sides. Queen Henrietta Maria, bringing reinforcements to the king in July 1643, wrote from Walsall: 'I shall stay here tomorrow because our soldiers are very weary and also because they have got so much plunder they cannot well march with their bundles'. Dame Joyce Blundell complained in a petition after the Restoration that as she was travelling through Lichfield during the war the royalist governor of Lichfield garrison, Colonel Richard Bagot, seized all her plate, valued at £2,000, on the pretence that the garrison would mutiny for want of pay.

On 16, 17 and 18 September 1642 Charles and his army marched through Staffordshire en route to Shrewsbury, where he hoped to gain more support than had been forthcoming in the Midlands. He spent a

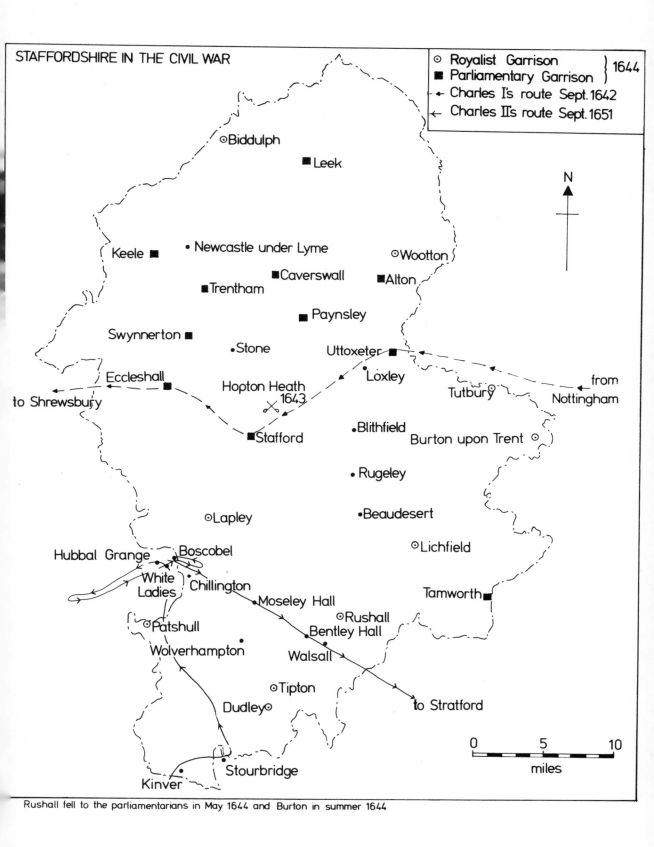

# STAFFORDSHIRE IN THE CIVIL WAR

| | |
|---|---|
| ⊙ | Royalist Garrison |
| ■ | Parliamentary Garrison |
| ← | Charles I's route Sept. 1642 |
| ← | Charles II's route Sept. 1651 |

1644

N

⊙Biddulph

■Leek

Keele■

• Newcastle under Lyme

⊙Wootton

•Caverswall

■Alton

■Trentham

•Paynsley

Swynnerton■

•Stone

Uttoxeter■

from Nottingham

•Loxley

Eccleshall■

Tutbury⊙

to Shrewsbury

Hopton Heath
1643

•Blithfield

Burton upon Trent ⊙

■Stafford

•Rugeley

•Beaudesert

⊙Lapley

⊙Lichfield

Hubbal Grange    •Boscobel

Tamworth■

White Ladies    •Chillington

•Moseley Hall

⊙Patshull

⊙Rushall
Bentley Hall

Wolverhampton

Walsall

to Stratford

⊙Tipton

Dudley⊙

Kinver    •Stourbridge

0    5    10
miles

Rushall fell to the parliamentarians in May 1644 and Burton in summer 1644

night at Tutbury Castle, one of the prisons of his grandmother, Mary Queen of Scots, and then proceeded via Uttoxeter to Stafford. His progress through the county roused more clamour than recruits. At Uttoxeter Prince Rupert burnt the houses of some who had refused to join the royal army. The king had a more encouraging reception at Stafford. At Shrewsbury his forces were reinforced by Welsh levies, and on 12 October the king began his march to London. His army, then 16,000 strong, moved through South Staffordshire. On 15 October Charles arrived at Wolverhampton, where the inhabitants were reported to have responded generously to his appeal for financial aid. There was, nevertheless, some plundering of the town and the surrounding area until, after three nights, the king moved on.

Dudley Castle, Tamworth, Lichfield Close and Stafford were seized by royalists in the autumn of 1642 as points from which they could attack parliament's supply lines. A few royalist gentlemen like Peter Giffard of Chillington also fortified and garrisoned their houses. Royalist troops occupied Tutbury Castle late in 1642. Nearby Burton changed hands a number of times during the war, its bridge over the Trent, the only one for miles, being of considerable strategic importance. The Moorlands area was controlled for parliament by Sir John Bowyer of Knypersley, though there was a royalist garrison at Biddulph. In the north-west of the county the Sneyds of Keele opted for the king and garrisoned their hall, though by February 1643 it had fallen to parliament. The first parliamentary success in Staffordshire was the capture of Lichfield Close on 5 March 1643. William Dugdale, an historian with royalist sympathies, recorded the activities of the parliamentary soldiers in the cathedral:

> They stabled their horses in the body of it, kept courts of guards in the cross aisles, broke up the pavements, polluted the choir with their excrement, every day hunted a cat with hounds throughout the church, delighting themselves in the echo from the goodly vaulted roof, and to add to their wickedness, brought a calf into it, wrapped in linen, carried it to the font, sprinkled it with holy water and gave it a name in scorn and derision of the holy sacrament of baptism.

*Spencer Compton,*
*earl of Northampton*

The parliamentary forces did not hold the Close for long. On 20 April Prince Rupert, using mining techniques learnt in his soldiering on the Continent, breached the defences and regained the Close. The royalists then held it until the end of the war.

The royalist troops had been allowed to march out of Lichfield when it surrendered. They made their way to Stafford, where they were joined by the earl of Northampton, whose troops had arrived at Lichfield too late to prevent its surrender. Stafford's importance as the county town and as a strategic centre prompted Sir John Gell,

26. Alton Castle. (*Photograph by Ken Sheridan; Staffordshire County Council Planning and Development Department.*)

27. The gardens at Alton Towers. (*Photograph by Stan Gruszewicz; Staffordshire County Council Planning and Development Department.*)

34. The Abbots Bromley horn dance at Blithfield Hall. (*Peter Rogers, Stafford.*)

35. Thor's Cave from the Manifold Valley. (*Photograph by Ken Sheridan; Staffordshire County Council Planning and Development Department.*)

commander of the parliamentary forces in Derbyshire, and Sir William Brereton, commanding in Cheshire, to plan an assault on the town. They agreed to meet at Hopton Heath, about two and a half miles from Stafford. Gell arrived at the rendezvous on the morning of 19 March 1643 and was joined in the afternoon by Brereton's horse. Before the latter's foot arrived the royalists attacked. The opposing forces have been estimated at 1,850 men for parliament and 1,200 for the king. Though the earl of Northampton was killed, the royalist horse, superior in numbers and experience, overwhelmed Gell's cavalry, and their 29-pounder cannon—'Roaring Meg'—inflicted heavy damage on the parliamentary infantry. The day was saved for parliament by the arrival of Brereton's foot, and with night falling the royalists had to disengage. Brereton and Gell ordered a general withdrawal of their forces during the night.

*Tixall Hall, home of the royalist Aston family: the gatehouse*

The royalists did not, however, retain Stafford much longer. On the night of 16 May a few picked parliamentary troops made their way undiscovered into the town, 'the people being quiet in their beds', as Brereton reported; the town was captured and many prisoners were taken. At Stafford Castle the dowager Lady Stafford offered stout resistance to the parliamentary forces for some time with the aid of complex defensive works.

Parliament captured Tamworth in the summer of 1643, and Eccleshall Castle, a seat of the bishop of Coventry and Lichfield, and also a royalist garrison, fell to parliamentary assault on 30 August after an eight weeks' siege. The besiegers found a trunk full of plate, 40 barrels of beer, and the body of the bishop who had died during the siege. This success for parliament was offset by royalist victories; Leek fell to the king on 28 November 1643 and Lapley House on 21 December. Pressure on the parliamentary forces in Staffordshire was relieved by the defeat inflicted on the royalists at the battle of Nantwich, in Cheshire, on 25 January 1644. Another parliamentary success was the capture of Burton upon Trent in the spring of 1644. The rejoicings of that mainly anti-royalist town were marred by the explosion of two barrels of gunpowder stored in the church, which did considerable damage to the building. On 12 June 1644 there was a sharp action between parliamentary troops seeking to renew the siege of Dudley Castle and a relieving royalist force. The parliamentarians remained masters of the field but were unable to resume the siege.

In the late summer of 1643 the earl of Denbigh, the parliamentary commander in the Midlands, fell under suspicion of having neutralist sympathies. Though the House of Lords cleared him of the charge, he was relieved of his command and there was a purge of Midland commanders loyal to him. On 3 December 1644 Gell and Brereton entered Stafford and arrested Colonel Lewis Chadwick, the governor of the town, and other officers. Chadwick was replaced by Captain Henry Stone of Walsall, whose militant views met with more approval by the parliamentary authorities.

The tide of war turned decisively in favour of parliament with its victory at Marston Moor, in Yorkshire, on 2 July 1644. In Staffordshire parliamentary forces began more systematic attacks on royalist garrisons. Gell raided Tutbury Castle on 6 July 1644. Later that month the royalists, who had reoccupied Burton upon Trent, were evicted from that town, and a permanent parliamentary garrison was installed there. In the spring of 1645 Charles left Oxford and marched northwest to relieve Chester as a first step in the reconquest of the north of England. His route took him through Himley and Bushbury and along the western boundary of Staffordshire towards Market Drayton in Shropshire. News reached him that parliament had abandoned its siege of Chester and that its troops were advancing on Oxford. Charles decided to delay his possible reconquest of the north and ordered his forces in the West Country and South Wales to meet him at Leicester. He passed through Stone, Uttoxeter, Tutbury and Burton upon Trent en route to the rendezvous. Charles's reinforcements failed to arrive, and the battle of Naseby, in Northamptonshire, fought on 14 June 1645, was a decisive victory for parliament. The king led the remnants of his army back to Hereford, passing through Lichfield and Wolverhampton.

By the end of 1645 only the south-west of Staffordshire and Dudley Castle remained under royalist control, and there was little point in further resistance. At the end of April 1646 the royalist garrison at Tutbury, affected by plague, surrendered, and Dudley Castle capitulated on 13 May. Lichfield was the last of the royalist garrisons in the county to surrender. Despite the king's instructions to capitulate the garrison continued to resist. Brereton bombarded the cathedral and its central spire was destroyed, Brereton concluding 'that this downfall would also humble their lofty proud spirits in the Close'. On 10 July the garrison commander, convinced at last that there was no hope of relief, surrendered on honourable terms.

Charles II endeavoured to recover his throne in 1651 when he invaded England with a Scottish army. He was defeated at the battle of Worcester on 3 September and fled north. On 4 September he came through the south-western corner of Staffordshire on his way to Whiteladies House, just over the border in Shropshire. Whiteladies was occupied by the Penderel family, tenants of the Giffards of Chillington. Charles Giffard, who was in the royal party, owned nearby Boscobel. After a vain attempt to escape westwards across the river

*Charles II escaping from Staffordshire, accompanied by Jane Lane*

Severn Charles returned to Boscobel and spent the day of 6 September hiding in an oak tree near the house. At nightfall he and one companion began to walk the seven miles to Moseley Hall, the home of Thomas Whitgreave, but he collapsed en route. He was taken back to Boscobel, horses were obtained, and this time he rode to Moseley. From there he went to Bentley Hall near Willenhall, the home of Colonel John Lane, and finally, disguised as a servant, with Jane, the colonel's daughter, riding pillion behind him, he escaped south, via Stratford, to Bristol.

*Thomas Harrison*

The consequences of the war for the king's supporters in Staffordshire were serious. Parliament admitted of no neutrality, and all estates were confiscated unless the owner was known to be favourable to parliament's cause. Confiscated lands could, however, be recovered on payment of a fine, assessed according to the offender's degree of delinquency. For example, a royalist who had been actively in arms against parliament was fined more heavily than one who had been a more passive supporter. Thus Sir Richard Leveson of Trentham, the governor of Dudley Castle, was fined £9,846, to be reduced to £6,000 if he settled the income from various tithes on certain church livings in the county. Many royalists ran into debt in recovering their lands. Nevertheless, the larger royalist landowners suffered no great loss of land as a result of the Civil War.

Staffordshire was affected by the constitutional and religious changes that came with the Interregnum. Its parliamentary representation was reduced from ten to six M.P.s in 1653, though in 1659 it was restored to its former number. There is some evidence of an attempt to enforce a Puritan code of social behaviour on the inhabitants of Staffordshire during the military rule of the major-generals. In 1655 John Jackson, the vicar of Lapley, petitioned the county justices to suppress wakes weeks, the greater part of which, he alleged, were spent in 'promiscuous dancing, morris dancing, tippling, gaming, quarrelling, wantonness . . . And thus they run on in the breach of every command of God against the reformation engaged, to the pulling down common calamity upon the country'. During the period there was an increase in the stipends of some of the more poorly-paid clergy. One of the livings which Sir Richard Leveson had to augment was Barlaston; in 1646 he was ordered to settle £35 per annum out of the impropriated rectorial tithes on the curate. Many of the livings in the county were filled by ministers of Puritan convictions, and at the Restoration at least 44 Staffordshire clergymen were ejected.

There were two regicides associated with Staffordshire. John Bradshaw, M.P. for Stafford and Cheshire in 1654 and steward of Newcastle under Lyme from 1641 until his death in 1659, was the president of the court which tried Charles I and sentenced him to death. Thomas Harrison, son of Richard Harrison, a butcher and four times mayor of Newcastle under Lyme, was appointed a major-general in the parliamentary army in 1648. He was a Fifth Monarchy Man, who expected the imminent return to earth of Christ, for which it was the task of believers to prepare society. He was among the first to sign the death warrant for the king's execution. On Charles II's return in 1660 Harrison was brought to trial; he was hanged, drawn and quartered at Charing Cross.

Charles II received many petitions from royalists seeking reward for their services or compensation for their sacrifices. Among those who obtained some recognition were members of the Penderel family, who received pensions, and the Lanes, who received, with other rewards, the right to augment the family coat of arms with part of the royal arms. The Bagots of Blithfield did relatively well: Hervey Bagot received a commission in the Life Guards, and his daughter Mary, later countess of Falmouth, was made lady-in-waiting to the duchess of York. There were too many claims from royalist sufferers, however, for Charles to satisfy more than a few. A letter of 1675 from Lord Aston of Tixall sounded a note of bitterness which was shared by many:

> I have often ventured my life and all that was dear to me in express-ing my loyalty. I have under his late Majesty's hand these words, 'Lord Aston, the greatest of my misfortunes is that I cannot reward so gallant and loyal a subject as you are, as I would and ought' . . . I have that pride not to bear with patience abiding in a country where my family has been eminent 20 descents and bore always places of trust under their kings, now to be trampled on and falsely accused by such as, till their fighting against the king and buying the estates of his loyal subjects, were not the least known.

*Moseley Hall*

# IX  Elections and Party Politics

Staffordshire's parliamentary history is characteristic of that of English provinces generally: sparse and irregular representation in the Middle Ages, a revival of borough representation in Tudor times, a variety of borough franchises, the existence of pocket boroughs, an increase in the number of seats in the 19th century, and a growth in support for the Labour Party in the 20th century.

Staffordshire returned two knights of the shire to parliament in 1258. Lichfield was considered to be sufficiently important to be one of the English towns represented at a special council in 1268, but it first returned to parliament in 1305. Tamworth was included in the sheriff of Warwickshire's return for 1275, but whether any of the Staffordshire towns was represented in that year is not known. Stafford was represented by two burgesses in the parliament of 1295, and thereafter its representation was fairly continuous. The first burgesses for Newcastle under Lyme were returned for the parliament of 1354 and fairly regularly afterwards. Borough representation in medieval parliaments was often irregular as the sheriff was free to decide which towns he would instruct to return members. Thus Lichfield's representation was intermittent from 1305 to 1353; it then lapsed, to be revived 200 years later in 1548. After 1275 Tamworth did not return to parliament until 1563. By the early years of Elizabeth I's reign the total representation of the county was 10— two knights of the shire, and two burgesses for each of the four parliamentary boroughs. Staffordshire's representation remained at that figure until the reforms of the 19th century, apart from a temporary reduction during the Commonwealth. By the Instrument of Government of 1653 the county was given one more member, Lichfield, Stafford and Newcastle under Lyme lost one member each, and Tamworth lost its separate representation altogether. Thus there were only six M.P.s for the county in the parliaments of 1654-5 and 1656-8. The parliament of 1659, after Cromwell's death, was called on the basis of the old system, and the county's representation rose again to 10, a figure at which it remained until 1832.

The medieval knights of the shire were usually county gentry, like Sir John Bagot of Blithfield, who sat for the county eight times between 1391 and 1421. The county franchise, by an Act of 1430, lay in persons holding freehold land worth at least 40 shillings a year.

*Arms of the Bagot family, 1583*

69

*Walter Chetwynd, M.P. for Stafford 1674-9 and 1685-7 and for Staffordshire 1690-3*

Early election procedure was loose; there was no list of electors, and the election was made by popular acclamation or show of hands. The 40-shilling freehold remained the formal qualification until 1832, though in time the term acquired a wider connotation and came to include schoolmasters, parsons, annuitants, and many others.

In the boroughs the right to vote went by custom, with a tendency to restrict the franchise to members of the borough councils. Thus at Newcastle under Lyme in 1624 the election was made by the mayor, the bailiffs, the aldermen and the capital burgesses. The defeated candidate petitioned the House of Commons, and in the report on that petition it was stated that in the time of Edward IV (1461–83) all the burgesses of the town had voted. A new election was held on that basis, and thereafter the right of all the burgesses to vote went unchallenged. Borough M.P.s were at first burgesses, but in the 15th century an increasing number of county gentry began to sit for the boroughs as the prestige of a seat in parliament grew. Walter Chetwynd of Ingestre was returned for Stafford in 1491, and thereafter his descendants frequently represented the borough up to the late 18th century.

The influence of the gentry helped eventually to break the monopoly of the franchise enjoyed by the borough councils. At Tamworth, in the election of 1669, John Ferrers obtained a majority of the votes by calling in the 'common inhabitants' to the poll, when his opponent, Lord Clifford, had secured the votes of the members of the corporation. Clifford petitioned against the result, arguing for a restricted interpretation of the term 'Commonalty' used in the charter of incorporation of 1560:

> The admitting of the word Commonalty to imply the inhabitants would make them of equal authority and trust with the Bailiffs and Capital Burgesses, the consequences whereof would somewhat resemble anarchy.

He won his petition and Ferrers was unseated. In 1698, however, the House of Commons determined that the right to vote lay with those who paid scot and lot—church and poor rates. This produced an electorate in Tamworth of about 250 in the mid 18th century. In Stafford the franchise according to the determination of 1721 lay with members of the corporation and the resident freemen, that is, those who by apprenticeship, inheritance or purchase had been admitted to the freedom of the borough. There were about 400 electors in 1722. The 1624 determination that the right to vote in Newcastle lay with all the burgesses was reaffirmed in 1704 and 1706, and resulted in an electorate there of about 440 in 1724. At Lichfield the franchise was mixed: by the determination of 1718 it included 40-shilling freeholders, enrolled freemen paying scot and lot, and burgage tenants. In 1753 there were 609 voters in the borough.

70

A statute of 1696 endeavoured to tighten election procedure, but sharp practice continued. Thus Thomas Clark, the defeated candidate in the election at Lichfield in 1722, complained that the returning officer had been prevailed upon by the other candidates to hold the election 14 days early, 'by which means most of the electors were deprived of giving their votes and the petitioner of being elected'. The widening of the franchise had not, in fact, produced freer elections in the boroughs, all four of which were in the 18th century under the control or influence of local patrons. The Leveson-Gower family's influence in Newcastle began with the election of William Leveson-Gower in 1675. From 1747 the family was able to nominate for both the Newcastle seats. Its methods of borough control were numerous. It regulated admission to the freemen's roll—the electoral register—through its influence over the corporation, ensured by hospitality at Trentham Hall, by leasing houses to members of the corporation at low rents, by paying the borough's debts, and by gifts which relieved the corporation of the unpopularity of imposing a poor rate. The voters themselves were influenced in a number of ways. In 1790 there were 131 voters—more than 22 per cent. of the total electorate—living in houses owned by the Leveson-Gowers, and some tenants lived rent-free for years. Such tenants who 'disobliged' their landlord at the hustings were liable to be evicted, as occurred after the 1734 election. Leveson-Gower control of the borough, however, depended not only on such forms of pressure on the electorate, but also on political apathy and a sense of loyalty and obligation to the family among the borough inhabitants.

With the development of the movement for parliamentary reform in the late 18th century and the widening of the electorate as a result of population growth, the Leveson-Gower hold on Newcastle began to weaken. A local family, the Fletcher-Bougheys of Betley, led the attack. A broadsheet of 1790 satirised Leveson-Gower influence thus:

> And the Lord called his steward of the household and said unto him,
> Behold the time is come that there will be a general election throughout
> the land and I will send my kinsman and my son-in-law to our old
> borough . . . and shall say unto the people, these are the chosen of
> the Lord.

*John Leveson-Gower,
1st Earl Gower (d. 1754)*

The Leveson-Gowers staved off the attack for some years by using their influence with the corporation to create 'tow-heads'—freemen made for electoral purposes. In 1814 the family took the decision to require full payment of rents in Newcastle. The consequent unpopularity and the financial burden of maintaining an electoral influence prompted the family to sell most of its property in Newcastle in 1825 and to end its involvement in the politics of that borough.

Stafford broke free from the Chetwynds' influence after 1770, but the electorate became more openly corrupt. Richard Brinsley Sheridan, the playwright, who sat for the borough from 1780 to 1806, was said to have initiated the practice of paying five guineas to each burgess at election time. Lichfield remained longer under the control of patrons. Lord Gower and Thomas Anson of Shugborough began to buy up burgage tenements from 1745 and let them to compliant voters. There was a series of bitterly-contested elections between the Gower–Anson alliance and local Tory gentry, that of 1747 rumoured to have cost Gower and Anson £20,000. By 1768, however, their influence was sufficiently well-established to deter the local opposition from contesting the election of that year, and there were no further contests until 1799. The Gower–Anson interest remained dominant in Lichfield until the Reform Act of 1832. The parliamentary interest at Tamworth in the second half of the 18th century was also shared between two patrons, Thomas Thynne, 1st Viscount Weymouth (later Marquess of Bath) of Drayton Bassett, and George Townshend, Viscount and later Marquess Townshend, of Tamworth Castle. 'Castle' and 'Manor' monopolised the borough representation from 1765 until after the Reform Act of 1832. Robert Peel the elder bought the Weymouth property in 1790, and his son Robert was M.P. for Tamworth from 1830 to 1850 and twice prime minister.

To avoid the expense of contested elections the gentry normally arranged among themselves who should represent the county. In 1747, however, a contest was brought on by a split in their ranks. The occasion was the resentment felt by the Tory squires of Staffordshire, by reputation a strongly Jacobite county, at the behaviour of Lord Gower. Gower, a leading Jacobite in 1715, had in 1742 gone over to the Hanoverians by joining the Whig government. Dr. Johnson, himself a native of Lichfield, recalled the Tories' disapproval in a conversation about his *Dictionary* with James Boswell in 1777:

> You know, Sir, Lord Gower forsook the old Jacobite interest. When I came to the word Renegade, after telling that it meant one who deserts to the enemy, a revolter, I added: 'Sometimes we say a Gower'. Thus it went to the press, but the printer had more wit than I and struck it out.

Gower went further and raised a regiment to fight against the Young Pretender in the rebellion of 1745, an action which brought him an earldom, but also the opposition of the Tories in the county election of 1747. Two Tories, Sir Walter Wagstaffe Bagot and John Crewe, stood against the two Gower nominees, William Leveson-Gower, the earl's brother, and Sir Richard Wrottesley, his son-in-law. There was a hard-fought contest which lasted six days and cost the Tory candidates

*Staffordshire pottery figure of Sir Robert Peel (about 1850)*

72

alone £4,540, mostly in bills for food and drink at the public houses. The result was a draw; Bagot obtained one seat and Gower the other. A few weeks later at Lichfield, where the Whigs had unseated the Tories, the duke of Bedford, Gower's son-in-law, was attacked on the racecourse. For all Staffordshire's Jacobite reputation, none of the county gentry rallied to the Pretender's cause in 1745 despite the fact that he marched through the north-east of the county en route to Derby. With the accession of George III to the throne in 1760 much of the antipathy to the Hanoverians disappeared: Horace Walpole noted that even Sir Walter Wagstaffe Bagot appeared at Court.

*Engraving showing the assault on the duke of Bedford on Lichfield racecourse after the election of 1747*

There were no further contests for the county seats until 1832. By the Reform Act of that year Staffordshire's representation was increased from 10 to 17 members. The county was divided into northern and southern constituencies, with two members each; Stoke and Wolverhampton were enfranchised, each with two members, and Walsall received one. The electorates were slightly increased, Newcastle's voters rising in number from 828 to 973, of whom 246 were the newly-enfranchised £10 householders. The Reform Act produced little immediate change in the nature of elections in the county and in the older boroughs. Open corruption was still practised. One of the candidates for the election at Stafford in 1832 entered the town preceded by a band with bank notes stuck in the front of their hats. Only the dissolution of parliament in 1834 saved the borough from being disfranchised for such proceedings. Nor did the influence of the local gentry diminish rapidly. Until the introduction of the secret ballot in 1872 voters could still be influenced, and the local power of such people as Richard Dyott at Lichfield and the Whig duke of Sutherland and the Tory Lord Ward in the county generally was a decisive·factor in elections. In 1869 both members elected for Stafford in 1868 were unseated, the Liberal for intimidation, the Conservative for corruption.

The period following the Reform Act of 1832 saw the beginnings of party organisation in Staffordshire. By 1836 a Conservative Association covered the south of the county. Its finances were handled by William Salt (whose collection of Staffordshire historical material became the foundation of the William Salt Library at Stafford). In 1837 the Whigs established a County Reform Association at a meeting at Trentham Hall. Both parties had formed borough associations by 1840. The full development of their organisations did not come, however, until after the widening of the franchise by the Reform Acts of 1867 and 1884.

The Reform Acts of 1867 increased Staffordshire's representation to nineteen. The county was given three divisions with two members each; a new borough, Wednesbury, was created, with one member, while Lichfield lost one of its representatives. The electorate was nearly doubled. There was a further extension of the franchise in 1884, followed by a systematic redistribution of seats on the basis of population by an Act of 1885. Newcastle under Lyme, Stafford and Stoke upon Trent each lost one member; Lichfield and Tamworth lost their separate representation; Wolverhampton gained another seat; and two new boroughs, Hanley and West Bromwich, were created; the county's total representation was thus seventeen. Further changes in the number and boundaries of the constituencies were made in 1918 and 1944. In the 1945 election there were 18 seats to be contested.

At first Liberals dominated in the industrial north and south of the county. Between 1832 and 1880 they gained 17 of the 28 seats in Stoke upon Trent. After 1885 they gained more working-class and trade-union support and won all three of the elections in the Potteries in 1912. Liberals won a share of the county representation in the 19th century, but from 1910 Conservatives tended to replace Liberals in the county seats and in the semi-rural constituencies.

Working-class radicalism expressed itself in the Potteries in the Chartist riots of 1842. The riots provoked a strong reaction from the authorities, and 56 men from North Staffordshire were transported overseas for penal labour. Joseph Capper, a blacksmith from Tunstall and a Primitive Methodist preacher, was sentenced to two years' imprisonment, which he served in Stafford gaol. For some time thereafter the political thrust of the working classes was channelled through the Liberal Party. One of the first working-class M.P.s was Alexander MacDonald, a miners' leader standing as a Liberal, who was returned for Stafford in 1874 with the help of the boot and shoe operatives in the town. Local Labour parties began to be formed after 1906 in the Potteries, and by 1910 there was a section of the Independent Labour Party in the area. At first working-class voters were content to support 'Lib–Lab' candidates such as John Ward, who was consistently returned for Stoke upon Trent from 1906 to 1924. The first successful Labour Party candidate in the Potteries was Samuel Finney, a miner and a trade union official, returned for the newly-created constituency of Burslem in 1918. From 1935 all three Potteries constituences were safe Labour seats. A similar pattern can be seen in the Black Country. In the Smethwick election of 1918 there was a cross-current when the suffragette Christabel Pankhurst contested the seat, which was won by the Labour candidate. From 1926 to 1931 Oswald Mosley (from 1928 Sir Oswald) sat for the borough, first as a Labour Party member and then from March to October 1931 representing his own New Party. The Conservative Party held the seat from 1931 to 1945 when it was captured by Labour. Yet another cross-current

*Alexander MacDonald*

74

at Smethwick was evident in 1964, when a Conservative ousted the long-standing Labour member, Patrick Gordon-Walker; by then the issues included the question of Commonwealth immigration into the area.

*Chartley Hall, home of Robert Devereux, earl of Essex, who nominated over half of Staffordshire's M.P.s in 1592*

# X The Land

*Drawing of the earl of Derby on a grant of pasture and pannage in Needwood forest in 1253*

Until the Industrial Revolution, the great majority of the inhabitants of Staffordshire got their living from the land. The main agricultural area has always been the well watered, comparatively low-lying central part of the county. It was the chief source of such prosperity as the county knew until the 18th century, when the emphasis shifted dramatically to the new and growing industrial centres of North and South Staffordshire. Yet although the towns absorbed land and labour, they also provided markets for agricultural produce and cattle. Most of the land in the county has continued to be devoted to farming: in 1973 nearly 70 per cent. was under cultivation, and there were some 6,000 farmers.

In 1086 Domesday Book revealed a poor and thinly-populated county with subsistence agriculture. There was still extensive woodland and waste, much of it within the forests. Nevertheless those unploughed tracts played an important part in the rural economy, for they provided the peasants with pasture for their cattle and pigs, and with timber for building and fuel. Needwood forest was extensively used for pasture by the neighbouring villages which had grown up on the more favourable land along the Trent and Dove.

During the next 200 years Staffordshire shared in the general expansion of agriculture as population and settlements increased, more land was brought into cultivation, and numerous local markets were established. At Brewood 51 inhabitants were recorded in 1086; in 1298 there were some 30 free tenants and tenants of new land, 29 tenants of burgages and 98 unfree tenants. At Cannock 14 inhabitants were recorded in 1086, and at Rugeley nine; each had 90 peasant tenants in 1298. Eccleshall in the same period experienced a five-fold increase to some 500 inhabitants. The process of *assarting,* or bringing new land into cultivation, was in progress by the 12th century. The lords of manors—and the Crown in the case of the forests—often permitted encroachments in return for fines and rents; often the lords were themselves responsible for the process. In 1155 the king granted the bishop 1,500 acres assarted around Lichfield and Brewood since 1135, evidently out of Cannock forest; the bishop seems to have paid £100 for the grant. The Augustinian priory at Ranton, west of Stafford, founded about 1150 by Robert, son of Noel, lord of the nearby Ellenhall, was evidently built on cleared land, being known as the priory of St Mary of the Assarts. Humbler people joined in: an assart made by Siward the cobbler in the bishop's manor of Brewood was recorded about the mid 12th century. Many lords, notably in the 13th century, founded new settlements as commerical speculations in the form of boroughs where the burgage tenements were held on favourable terms to attract settlers. Some boroughs prospered and became towns, like Walsall, Uttoxeter and Burton; others remained villages, like Kinver, Brewood, Eccleshall, and Abbots Bromley.

The religious orders played an important part in the improvement of agriculture, especially the Cistercians who in the 12th and 13th centuries settled in remote parts and proceeded to develop them, especially for sheep farming. In Staffordshire such activity was to be found particularly in the Moorlands of the north-east where in the late 13th century Croxden abbey had some 7,200 sheep, and Dieulacres some 4,800. The Benedictines of Burton were then the second largest wool producers in the county with some 6,000 sheep. Several Staffordshire monasteries were exporting wool—not only the Cistercians and Benedictines, but also the Augustinians of Rocester and Trentham. The Templars had 260 sheep at Keele in 1308, while in 1322 Tutbury priory had 376 sheep and 100 lambs at Mayfield. The religious were also involved in stock farming, Burton abbey having large herds of cows in the early 12th century.

The rich grasslands of central Staffordshire and the heaths of Cannock forest also supported cattle. The bishop had substantial dairy herds on his manors there in 1298, notably at Haywood; a few years later he also had large flocks of sheep. In the early 14th century Sir Robert de Holland, lord of Yoxall, kept a large dairy herd in Needwood forest.

The predominant method of farming which emerged in medieval Staffordshire—with local variations—was that associated with open arable fields and meadows; the farmers within a manor had strips scattered in two or more fields, similar allotments in the meadows, and pasture and timber rights in the uncultivated land beyond. Crops were rotated annually, each field or part of it having a different crop on each sowing, or else being left fallow; after the crops had been gathered the land was given over to grazing. The system persisted long after the Middle Ages: in the late 18th century the south-east of the county had a rotation of fallow, wheat or barley, and pulse or oats. A map of c. 1725 for Marston, a manor to the north of Stafford, shows three open fields with each field sub-divided into blocks of strips. Nine farmers held strips in the fields. The largest holding was that of Thomas Greatbach, some 30 acres in extent. His strips were still scattered in all three fields, but he held several large groups of strips,

*Tithe barn at Mavesyn Ridware*

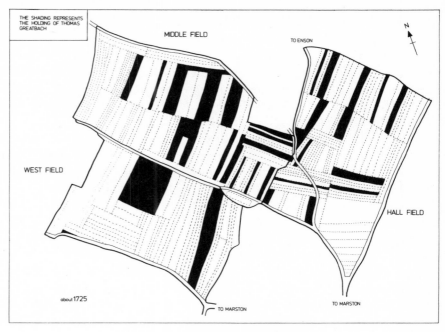

THE SHADING REPRESENTS THE HOLDING OF THOMAS GREATBACH

MIDDLE FIELD

TO ENSON

N

WEST FIELD

HALL FIELD

about 1725

TO MARSTON

TO MARSTON

*Plan of Marston Fields*

a sign of consolidation—the gathering of strips into compact groups by exchange with, or purchase from, other farmers. There was a much larger area of land in Marston which was held individually and not as part of the open fields; it probably represents assarted lands which had been brought under the plough after the creation of the three fields and never added to them.

The manorial structure which normally went with open-field farming—again with local variations—consisted of a lord, free tenants paying him rent, villein or unfree tenants owing extensive labour services on the lord's own land as well as rents and dues, and a labouring class which was landless or nearly so. The whole was managed by the manorial court, the workings of which can be traced in surviving court rolls. Those classes of tenant were in general the ones found on the estates of Burton abbey in the early 12th century. The services owed at various times of the year by the villeins of Sedgley in the 13th century were typical—reaping, mowing, hoeing, carrying hay and wood, gathering nuts, looking after the lord's animals. By then, however, it was becoming customary on many manors for the lord to take cash instead of services from his villeins. There were numerous examples of this on the Burton abbey estates in the early 12th century, and it was happening at Sedgley before 1300. In 1312-13 on the bishop's manor of Baswich near Stafford 40 acres

78

were harvested by customary labour and 99 acres by wage labour. A high proportion of free tenants was characteristic of Staffordshire about 1300; it reached 51 per cent. on the bishop's manors. On his manors of Cannock and Rugeley in 1298 there were no unfree tenants; on the other hand nearly two-thirds of the tenants were holding five acres or less, largely land assarted from the forest. At the other extreme services were still exacted by Lord Harrowby at Sandon as late as 1780.

*Timber-framed cottage at Mavesyn Ridware*

After the period of expansion the 14th century was one of crisis, with pressure on resources and many natural disasters. Staffordshire suffered during the famine which swept Europe between 1315 and 1317. The chronicle of Croxden abbey says of the year 1316 that it was 'memorable for dearness, famine, disease and death'. On the Burton abbey estates at Branston and Horninglow three people died of hunger in 1317. The Croxden chronicle says that the year 1319 brought 'a plague or murrain of animals unseen and unheard of hitherto'. At Keele in the 1320s land was lying out of use since tenants had fled because of poverty and there were too few animals for pasture to be needed. The Black Death reached Staffordshire in 1349. At Alrewas the court rolls record nearly 60 deaths in May, over 70 in June, some 50 in July, and some 12 in August. There was a second outbreak of plague in 1361.

Villages became deserted from the middle of the century, and before 1400 examples were to be found all over the county of land lying out of use, arable being used as pasture, and farm buildings fallen into ruin. As a result concessions were made to tenants to encourage repairs and improvements. At Pattingham in the south-west entry fines paid in the 1360s by tenants taking over property were reduced or even waived for those taking over uncultivated land or agreeing to repair ruinous buildings. Ruinous tenements were still a problem for the lord of Pattingham in the 1430s and 1440s, when reductions of rent were made to subsidise repairs. In the east of the county in the 1440s the duchy of Lancaster, too, was allowing subsidies for improvements on its estates.

Peasants were encouraged by the lords' difficulties to claim greater freedom. There was widespread refusal to accept the lord's monopoly of milling on the Burton abbey estates in the 1360s and at Pattingham in the 1380s. The decline of labour services was hastened. In the 1370s it was stated that the services due to the nuns of Farewell near Lichfield had not been performed since 1349. At Kinver at the end of the 14th century, the tenants refused to perform their labour services, which consisted of ploughing, mowing, haymaking, and carrying. The lord, John Hampton, agreed to take cash instead; his son, who succeeded him in 1433, confirmed the agreement in 1434.

Landlords attempted to recover their losses by leasing out more and more of the land which in the 13th century they had cultivated for profit. Those who continued to farm had to pay higher wages. In 1437-8 the earl of Stafford on his lands near Stafford paid 4d. a quarter for threshing, whereas in 1312-13 the bishop had paid 2d. at nearby Baswich; the rate for winnowing too had doubled. Stock farming increased, with Birmingham developing a cattle market which served South Staffordshire among other areas; Stafford, too, seems to have had a cattle market by the 15th century.

Another factor which steadily modified the early medieval pattern of farming was the gradual inclosure of the common arable and pasture—their withdrawal piecemeal or in their entirety from the communal system, and their conversion to individual use. Both lords and tenants were involved in the process in Staffordshire by the 13th century, often provoking violent opposition from those who wished to continue in the enjoyment of their common rights. From the later Middle Ages there was inclosure of arable throughout the kingdom for conversion into pasture for sheep, with consequent eviction of tenants. A government inquiry of 1517 shows that Staffordshire was not unduly affected. Since 1489 only 488 acres had been inclosed, most of it for pasture, and little eviction was recorded. At Chillington John Giffard inclosed five acres of arable in 1511 to make a park; his

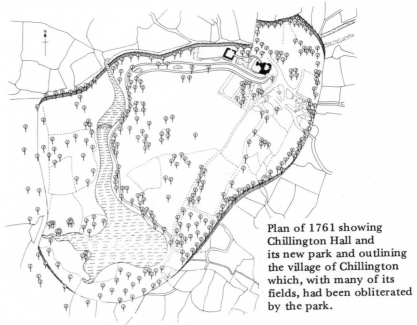

Plan of 1761 showing Chillington Hall and its new park and outlining the village of Chillington which, with many of its fields, had been obliterated by the park.

descendant, Thomas Giffard, went much further about 1760 when he obliterated the whole village of Chillington to allow the extension of his park. From the 16th century large tracts of forest land were being inclosed in the teeth of opposition from those enjoying common rights there. Thus in the 1630s John Whorwood of Stourton Castle fell foul of the local inhabitants when he inclosed part of Iverley common in Kinver forest and established a sheepcot there. When the commoners tried to graze their own sheep there Whorwood's servant set dogs on them. Attempts to inclose part of Needwood forest in the 17th century, notably under the Commonwealth, provoked fierce opposition and rioting on the part of the commoners.

A frequent method of inclosing arable fields was by agreement among the interested parties, as at Tunstall in 1613 when the nine freeholders divided the six open fields among themselves. Many Staffordshire villages had been so inclosed by 1700, and the process continued. Another method, not much used in Staffordshire, was by Act of Parliament. The first village in the county to be inclosed in that way was Elford in the south-east, where the four open fields and several meadows were inclosed in 1766 under an Act of 1765. The last area was Warslow and Lower Elkstone in the Moorlands in 1839. There were few open fields left by 1800, although as late as 1872 there was still some uninclosed arable at Sandon. Most of the Staffordshire Inclosure Acts were concerned with waste land. The biggest operation was the inclosure of Needwood forest (9,400 acres) in 1811 under an Act of 1801. In the 1860s some 3,000 acres of Cannock Chase was inclosed by Act.

Inclosure caused some hardship, especially among smaller tenants and cottagers who were dependent on vague rights of grazing and timber over large areas. When Needwood was inclosed John Allcock, a small proprietor in Marchington, lost all his common rights in the forest and received instead a meagre 2½-acre plot; for that he had to pay £11 as his share of the inclosure costs, and in addition he had to fence the plot at his own expense. Squatters, too, were affected. Among the benefits listed in the preamble to the Ipstones Inclosure Act of 1777 was the fact that inclosure would 'put a stop to many encroachments that are every day making upon the common by people who have no right to them and will keep many bad people out of the neighbourhood'. A similar view was expressed over the inclosure of Needwood: 'an extensive forest is not favourable to the virtue and industry of its poorer inhabitants; it affords temptations to idleness and dishonesty'.

On the whole, however, the effects of inclosure in Staffordshire do not seem to have been so severe as in other places. At Elford, for

*The Butter Cross at Abbots Bromley*

81

instance, it was claimed some 30 years after the inclosure that about 500 acres out of 1,900 were in tillage, bringing 'as much grain to market as the whole parish did in its open state; the quantity of cheese made now in proportion to that made prior to the inclosure is more than three to one; the proportion of beef and mutton produced on the lands is still greater, as much as ten to one'.

Cattle and dairy farming was important in the north-east by the late 17th century. Already about 1540 Leland had noted that the men of Uttoxeter 'useth grazing for there be wonderful pastures upon Dove'. Robert Plot extolled the grass of the Moorlands and the rich meadows along the rivers, above all the Dove which, flooding the meadows every spring, 'enriches them as the river Nile does Egypt and makes them so fruitful that the inhabitants thereabouts upon such occasions usually chant this joyful ditte: "In April Dove's flood is worth a king's good"'. The limestone hills and the meadows supported dairy farms which supplied so much good butter and cheese to the Uttoxeter market that the London cheesemongers had set up an agency there. With supplies coming from Derbyshire also the agents spent as much as £500 a day in the season. The butter was sold in long cylindrical pots made in Burslem and containing at least 14lb. Plot described the farmers' ruses of putting good butter on top and bad at the bottom and of filling only the top and leaving much of the rest empty; he also noted the counter-measures:

*A butter churn at Ivetsey Bank near Brewood*

> To prevent these little country moorlandish cheats (than whom no people whatever are esteemed more subtile) the factors keep a surveyor all the summer here, who, if he have ground to suspect any of the pots, tries them with an instrument of iron made like a cheese taster, only much larger and longer, called an auger or butterboare with which he takes proof (thrusting it in obliquely) to the bottom of the pot; so that they weigh none (which would be an endless business) or very seldom; nor do they bore it neither where they know their customer to be a constant fair dealer. But their cheese, which comes but little, if anything, short of that of Cheshire, they sell by weight as at other places.

In the late 18th century most of the land farmed in the county was still under the plough, and the Napoleonic Wars encouraged the extension of arable. Thereafter grassland farming developed. A government inquiry into cropping in 1801 revealed in Cannock parish, for example, nearly 2,000 acres sown; over three-quarters was with wheat, barley and oats, and the rest with peas, potatoes and turnips. Cannock, however, also had extensive pasture on the Chase: in 1819 there were 2,940 sheep being pastured there by people from Cannock parish, along with some cows, asses and horses. Grassland was coming to equal arable in area by the mid 19th century, and by the late 1860s

82

it had passed it. Arable then accounted for 230,000 acres, and grassland for 340,000 acres. By 1901 the difference had widened to 165,000 acres and 435,000 acres respectively.

The century saw a general improvement in the county's agriculture, the work of a number of improving landlords and their agents. By the 1860s the large Staffordshire landowners were considered to be the leaders in agricultural improvement among the great landowners of England; and Staffordshire was well above the national average in its proportion of large estates. The 1st Lord Hatherton at Teddesley, near Penkridge, was a notable improver. After succeeding to the property in 1812 he began draining and irrigating the gravelly soil, and by 1850 he had 1,700 acres producing wheat and barley and supporting 200 head of cattle and 2,000 head of Southdown sheep. From 1850 he was also running a free agricultural school on the estate where some 300 boys aged between 10 and 14 were educated, spending most of their time on the farm and the rest in 'educational pursuits'. In 1845 Lord Hatherton helped to form the Cannock Agricultural Association for tenant farmers in the area. Among the agents the most distinguished was James Loch, agent to the Leveson-Gowers from 1812 to 1855.

The continuing extension of grassland was halted in the present century by the need for increased food production during the two World Wars. From the 1960s barley was the main crop, followed at a distance by wheat, potatoes, oats and sugar beet. Grassland farming, however, remains predominant, with dairying the main element. In 1949–50 Staffordshire was the fourth largest milk-producing county with a production of 77 million gallons; by 1965 it was producing over 92 million gallons. Fattening for beef has been mainly a by-product of dairying, but beef production increased greatly from the late 1960s. Sheep farming has declined in the 20th century. The general pattern of farming is dairying in the northern upland, with some rearing of store cattle and sheep, mixed arable and also dairying in the central area, and arable with some dairying in the south. The present century has seen the break-up of the great estates matched by a growth in owner-occupation, which by 1970 accounted for 58½ per cent. of farms and 53½ per cent. of farmland.

*Stafford mill (demolished in 1957)*

Staffordshire is noted for two special breeds. The white Chartley cattle, possibly descended from the prehistoric Aurochs, are said to have been driven from Needwood forest into Chartley park by one of the earls of Derby in the 13th century. His successors at Chartley preserved them there in a semi-wild state. The herd averaged some 45 in the 1890s, but at the beginning of the 20th century it was nearly destroyed by disease. The survivors were crossed with Longhorn cattle.

*A Tamworth pig*

The new strain is no longer to be found in Staffordshire, but it survives elsewhere. The Tamworth pig, with its golden hair and pink skin, is thought to be a variant of the Berkshire breed, produced by crossing with imported stock, perhaps from India, in the early 19th century. Sir Francis Lawley of Middleton in Warwickshire, not far from Tamworth, and Sir Robert Peel of Drayton Bassett have each been credited with its introduction. Since the later 1970s it has been a feature of Shugborough Park Farm, part of the county museum at Shugborough.

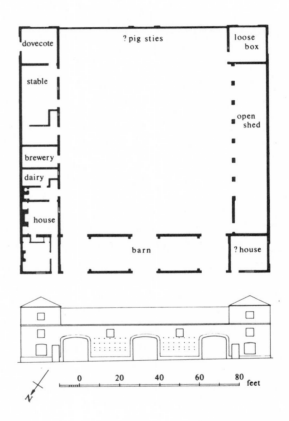

*The 18th-century Sandwell Park Farm, West Bromwich*

84

# XI  Potteries and Black Country

The idea common outside Staffordshire that the county is all Potteries and Black Country is a total misconception. It is, however, true that Staffordshire has been one of the main industrial areas of Britain since the 18th century. Indeed the pottery of North Staffordshire has given the county's name a world-wide currency, while South Staffordshire has been described as 'one great workshop' whose manufactures have been more varied than those of any similar area anywhere in the world.

*Cinerary urn of the mid-first century A.D. from Trent Vale*

The county had its industries long before the 18th century. Pottery was being made at Trent Vale soon after A.D. 50, and elsewhere coal, iron, clay, and building stone were being worked by the second century. In the Middle Ages there was widespread, if small-scale, industrial activity all over the county. Biddulph in North Staffordshire, a place-name recorded in 1086, is thought to mean 'the place by the mine'. There was ironstone mining and ironworking at Cheadle in the later 12th century. There were forges in Cannock forest by 1231, apparently in the Cannock and Rugeley area, and probably at Sedgley by 1273. Coalmining, too, was in progress side by side with ironstone mining at Tunstall and Sedgley by the later 13th century, and on Cannock Chase by 1298. Coal was being transported to Oxfordshire and Northamptonshire from the Finchpath area on the Wednesbury–West Bromwich boundary by the early 14th century. For centuries yet, however, the pits were only shallow workings in the outcrops, and coal was of secondary importance to charcoal in such a well-wooded county. In North Staffordshire there was pottery making, based on the local clay and quick-burning coal. Kilns dating from about 1300 have been discovered at Sneyd Green, near Burslem. Tiles were probably being made by the monks of nearby Hulton abbey in the 14th century.

The alabaster of the Tutbury area was being worked by the later 12th century; its use on the west doorway of the priory church at Tutbury about 1160–70 is the earliest known in England. The effigy of a knight in Hanbury church is probably that of Sir John de Hanbury, who died in 1303; if so, it is the earliest alabaster effigy in England. In 1374 John of Gaunt ordered six cartloads from his alabaster pits at Tutbury for his wife's tomb in St Paul's, London. There was a Staffordshire cloth industry before 1300, the earliest recorded fulling mill in the county being at Betley in the north-west in the 1270s.

By the mid-14th century the county had a glass industry of some repute, located probably in the area between Abbots Bromley and Rugeley. Staffordshire was one of the places from which in 1349 Edward III ordered the purchase of glass for St Stephen's chapel in Westminster Palace.

By Tudor times this activity had increased in scale and new industries had appeared. About 1540 the antiquary John Leland recorded that the smiths of Birmingham had 'iron out of Staffordshire and Warwickshire and sea coal out of Staffordshire'. At Walsall he noted coal and ironstone mining, limestone quarrying, and numerous makers of bits and spurs for horse-riding—the last was an industry which had become established in the town by the earlier 15th century. The school of alabaster carvers which Leland found at Burton upon Trent was also well over half a century old, and it survived into the 17th century; its products made their way overseas, and local examples include the fine tombs of the Littleton family in Penkridge church and of the Giffards at Brewood. Burton became well known for its ale in the 17th century; already in 1586 it was in barrels of Burton ale that the letters between Mary Queen of Scots at Chartley and the conspirators of the Babington Plot were smuggled. By the 1580s glassmakers from Lorraine who had settled in the Eccleshall area were bringing the Staffordshire glass industry a new importance. Early in the 17th century they moved to the Amblecote–Stourbridge area on the Staffordshire–Worcestershire boundary in the south-west, probably attracted by the availability of coal and also of a fireclay especially suited to the making of glasshouse pots. The district remains a centre of glassmaking.

*North Staffordshire slipware dish made by Ralph Toft about 1675 showing Catherine of Braganza, queen of Charles II*

The most notable advances in Tudor and Stuart times were in the iron industry, which was revolutionised by the introduction of the blast furnace. The furnace was replacing the bloomsmithy in the reign of Elizabeth I, and it seems that the first in the Midlands was that erected by William, 1st Baron Paget, at his ironworks on Cannock Chase in the early 1560s. A further advance came with the slitting mill, which brought about the mechanisation of the process of cutting rod iron into lengths for the nailers. Nailmaking had become a staple industry in the south of the county by the 1580s, and the earliest slitting mill recorded in the Midlands was that being worked by Thomas Chetwynd in 1623, probably at Rugeley. The mill established by Richard Foley at the Hyde in Kinver in the later 1620s seems to have been a great improvement on earlier versions. Soon afterwards Foley turned to the manufacture of iron, and his family continued as important ironmasters in many parts of the county and beyond until the 18th century.

When Robert Plot visited Staffordshire about 1680, he found the county well on its way to its later industrial pre-eminence. Pottery was produced in the south as well as the north, but the main centre was Burslem where the farmer-potters were engaged particularly in the production of butter pots for the Uttoxeter market. Clay pipes were made at Newcastle. Clay was also the basis of a brick and tile industry, again especially in the north. The mining of coal and ironstone was in progress all over the county, and copper was being mined at Ecton in the north. There was also widespread stone quarrying. Among the county's ironworkers there was at Keele one of the only two frying-pan makers in England. 'Prodigious numbers' of nailers in the south included 2,000 men and boys at Sedgley alone. Walsall was noted for 'ironworks . . . which chiefly relate to somewhat of horsemanship such as spurs, bridles, stirrups etc.' and also for copper and brass working, especially the making of buckles. Wolverhampton was a great centre of lockmaking, and edge tools were made along the rivers in the south-west of the county. A salt works had recently been established at Shirleywich, near Weston upon Trent, east of Stafford, so called from the family name (Shirley) of Lord Ferrers who owned the undertaking.

*Dish from Josiah Wedgwood's Russian dinner service with a view of Etruria Hall*

The complex of events in the 18th and 19th centuries known as the Industrial Revolution involved new techniques (notably the harnessing of steam power), the exploitation of new business methods, the gradual establishment of factories in place of domestic workshops, and a new system of communications. All those can be found in the achievements of the potter Josiah Wedgwood (1730–95). In 1769 he moved from Burslem to a new factory on a site in open country west of Hanley which he named Etruria, to give it the right Classical overtones. He also built a village there for his workers and a large house for himself overlooking the new works. Etruria was described in 1794 by the county's historian, Stebbing Shaw, as 'a colony newly raised where clay-built man subsists on clay'. To drive his clay, flint and colour mills Wedgwood installed steam engines. His experiments had already included a highly successful cream-coloured earthenware which he called Queensware. The name illustrated one of his business methods, the securing of the highest patronage—in this case the patronage of Queen Charlotte, wife of George III, which he won in 1765. In 1774 he completed another royal commission, a 952-piece dinner service in Queensware for the Empress Catherine II of Russia; it was decorated with views of English country houses and castles, including one of Etruria Hall. Wedgwood also led the movement for better communications and in the process brought turnpike roads and a canal to the Potteries—and to Etruria.

Wedgwood's part in the development of the pottery industry is well summarised by his epitaph in Stoke church—that he 'converted a rude and inconsiderable manufactory into an elegant art and an important part of national commerce'. There were, however, notable potters besides Wedgwood. His own family had long been potters in Burslem, where the Adams family, which was also to become an important pottery dynasty, was making pots in 1448. Wedgwood had been apprenticed to his brother Thomas at the family's Churchyard Works in Burslem, and from 1754 to 1758 he was in partnership with Thomas Whieldon, a distinguished potter of Fenton and an experimenter like Wedgwood. By 1762, when Wedgwood was only at the beginning of his career, there were already some 150 individual potteries in the Burslem area, employing about 7,000 people. Wedgwood never made porcelain, which was being produced by the Longton Hall Company in the 1750s. Bone china, a type of porcelain, was developed by Josiah Spode (1733–97) at Stoke upon Trent and by the potters of Longton, a town which grew up in the early 19th century as a centre of bone-china manufacture.

In the south of the county the great development was in the iron industry, based on local supplies of iron ore as raw material, coal as fuel, limestone as flux, and fireclay for building furnaces. The advance became possible when it was discovered how to smelt the ore with coal instead of charcoal, a discovery made by Abraham Darby, a native of the Dudley area working in Shropshire, who in 1709 introduced the necessary coking of coal. The great pioneer in Staffordshire was John Wilkinson (1728–1808), who erected the first of his Black Country furnaces at Bradley near Bilston in 1757-8, using coke smelting; soon afterwards he introduced steam power to provide the blast. There were 14 blast furnaces in the Black Country in 1796, producing 13,210 tons of pig iron; by 1815 there were 55 furnaces, and the output was some 115,000 tons. Technical advances continued, and the South Staffordshire iron trade reached its peak about 1870. By then local supplies of ore were having to be supplemented by ore from other parts of the country; competition from steel was also beginning. A decline set in.

North Staffordshire, too, had its iron industry, though on a smaller scale. The first coke blast furnace there was evidently one erected at Apedale, west of Newcastle, in 1768. Etruria became the main centre. Furnaces there belonging to Earl Granville were first blown in 1841, and the Wedgwood village became dominated by the works of the firm finally known as Shelton Iron and Steel Ltd., with its main office in the house built by Josiah. The scene has now changed once more with the closing of the works, and Etruria Hall stands gaunt and alone above a cleared landscape.

*John Wilkinson*

88

36. Working the Thick Coal in the South Staffordshire coalfield c.1890. (*Final Report of Miners' Eight Hour Day Committee, 1907.*)

37. Haden Hill colliery, Old Hill, in the late 19th century. The colliery belonged to the New British Iron Co. and supplied coal for the company's works at Cradley Heath. (*Photograph by C.W. Bassano; J.N. Cockin.*)

38.  Loading limestone from Caldon Low on to the Caldon Canal at Froghall in the late 19th century. (*Staffordshire County Museum.*)

39.  The footwear industry: the closing room at Lotus Ltd., Stafford, about 1930. (*Staffordshire County Museum.*)

Burton bridge from the south in 1839, looking across the Trent into Derbyshire. Drawing by J. Buckler. (*William Salt Library.*)

Galton bridge, Smethwick, built over the Birmingham Canal in 1828-9. Drawing by R. Bridgens. (*William Salt Library.*)

42. Toll house and gates at Littleworth, Stafford, at the junction of the Weston and Tixall roads before disturnpiking in 1878. (*Staffordshire County Museum and L. Robinson.*)

43. Alton station on the Churnet Valley line, opened in 1849. Watercolour drawing probably by L.J. Wood. (*William Salt Library.*)

The iron trade encouraged many ancillary industries, notably in South Staffordshire. The cottage nail industry received new encouragement, although from the 1820s it was gradually overtaken by machine-made nails, with factories replacing domestic workshops. The area also became a centre for the production of chains and anchors, the latter being introduced by Noah Hingley at his chain works in Netherton, near Dudley, in 1838. Wednesbury came to specialise in gun barrels, and when the demand declined after the end of the Napoleonic Wars the town turned to gas and water pipes; it became known as 'Tube Town'. Walsall also became a centre of the industry about 1830.

Engineering also was encouraged by the growth of the iron trade. A notable advance came in 1775 when James Watt, the genius of steam engineering, went into partnership with Matthew Boulton of the Soho Manufactory, a metal works in Handsworth. The factory produced its first steam engines in 1776—one for the Bloomfield colliery in Tipton, and the other for a furnace near Broseley in Shropshire owned by John Wilkinson. It was a cylinder invented by Wilkinson which made the Watt engine a commercial possibility. Another engine was built in the later 1770s for the Birmingham Canal Navigations to pump water from one canal level to another at Smethwick. It continued in use until the 1890s and was then moved to the canal maintenance depot at Ocker Hill in Tipton. It was dismantled in 1959 and installed in the Birmingham Museum of Science and Industry, where it remains, claimed as the oldest condensing engine in existence. In 1822 Tipton produced the first iron steamship, the *Aaron Manby,* named after its inventor. Engineering received a new impetus with the decline of the South Staffordshire iron trade in the later 19th century. The highly skilled work force of the area turned to new products like bicycles, cars and electrical apparatus and their components.

The development of the pottery and iron industries led to a corresponding growth in coalmining to meet their demands. This was aided by the new engines which were used to pump water out of mines and to sink new shafts. Thomas Newcomen erected his first engine in 1712, probably on a site in Tipton, north-west of Dudley castle. In South Staffordshire new mining areas were opened up—West Bromwich in the early 19th century is a notable example—and in the centre of the county the Cannock Chase coalfield developed rapidly from about 1850, creating a landscape which is neither town nor country. In the north the tendency was to deepen existing workings. The decline of the iron industry, exhaustion of coal seams, and flooding have brought mining to an end in the south, where the last colliery, Baggeridge in Sedgeley, closed in 1968. The Cannock Chase and North Staffordshire

*Silk weavers' cottages in London Road, Leek, built about 1825 with the workrooms on the top floor*

*Cheddleton flint mill*

fields remain important mining areas. Lea Hall, near Rugeley, which began production in 1960, was the first completely new mine opened by the National Coal Board. About the same time the Sutherland pit in Fenton, at 3,318 feet, was claimed to be the deepest in the country, with still deeper seams below the existing workings.

Other Staffordshire industries which developed in the later 18th and early 19th centuries included the silk industry at Leek, cotton spinning along the Dove, Trent and Tean, copper and brass working in the Cheadle and Wolverhampton areas. Willenhall joined Wolverhampton as a centre of lockmaking. Burton's brewing industry greatly expanded as communications improved, its beer reaching Russia in the 18th century and India in the early 19th century. At Stafford the boot and shoe industry developed rapidly, with Richard Brinsley Sheridan, M.P. for the borough from 1780 to 1806, proposing a toast at an election dinner with the words 'May the manufactures of Stafford be trodden under foot by all the world'. Brick and tile making was important in both north and south Staffordshire, with 'Staffordshire blue' engineering bricks a notable product. The pottery industry's use of flint produced numerous flint-grinding mills, notably in the Moddershall valley north of Stone; at Cheddleton, near Leek, a flint mill built by James Brindley about 1760 continued in use until 1963 and is now maintained by a trust. At the end of the 19th century a salt industry grew up in Stafford, and early in the 20th century the town also became a centre of electrical engineering.

It has been claimed that there is little which Staffordshire has not made, and the area of the old county remains a major industrial region with a wide range of products.

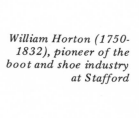

*William Horton (1750-1832), pioneer of the boot and shoe industry at Stafford*

90

# XII  Roads, Canals and Railways

Throughout its recorded history Staffordshire has been crossed by communications of national importance, and its development as a great industrial county from the 18th century was closely linked with the improvement of its system of communications. The Roman pattern of roads was extensively modified as new settlements and centres grew up. Thus in north-west Staffordshire in the Middle Ages the Roman fortress at Chesterton ceased to be a focal point, and the Anglo-Saxon church at Stoke and the 12th-century fortress at Newcastle became the new centres. The road from Derby no longer ran north-west from Fenton to Chesterton, therefore, but followed a more southerly course, crossing the Trent at Stoke and continuing over the high ground at Hartshill to Newcastle. On the other hand Rycknield Street in the east of the county remained important as the link between Lichfield and Burton. Henry III passed southwards along it in 1235, and finding the bridge over the Trent at Wychnor in a bad state, he assigned timber from Cannock forest for its repair.

*Watling Street with the Shropshire Union Canal aqueduct of 1832*

The most important of the medieval routes through the county was that from London to Chester, then the port for Ireland. The road entered the county in the south-east at Bassett's Pole, near Canwell, and ran through Lichfield and Rugeley to cross the Trent at Wolseley bridge. It then followed the Trent valley through Sandon to Stone, and from there it ran up the east bank of the river through Barlaston to Hanford. Continuing to Newcastle, it there turned west to Nantwich in Cheshire. Henry III took this road on his way to Chester and North Wales in 1257, stopping at Lichfield and Newcastle. The stretch through Barlaston was low-lying and liable to flood, and in the early 17th century the route was diverted to cross the Trent at Darlaston, near Stone, and run along the higher ground west of the river through Tittensor and Trentham. By the 1570s the Chester traffic was ceasing to go so far north as Newcastle, but swung north-west at Darlaston. The road to Newcastle, however, continued to be important as part of the route to Carlisle and Scotland. Beyond Newcastle it ran via Chesterton and Talke into Cheshire; its present more easterly course, by-passing those two places, dates from the 1820s.

Another route to Chester through the south of the county became popular after 1600. It left the other road near Coleshill in Warwickshire and ran via Castle Bromwich to Brownhills in Staffordshire where it

91

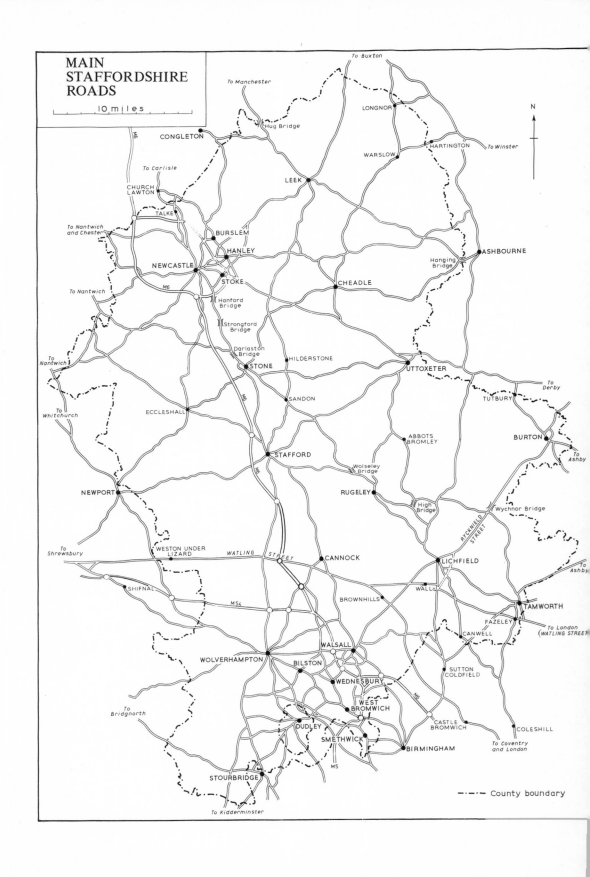

MAIN
STAFFORDSHIRE
ROADS

10 miles

joined Watling Street. It followed the Roman road to the Shropshire boundary and there branched north-west to Newport. Its advantage over the first route was that it passed through fewer towns and also had fewer river crossings.

*Toll house at Ipstones*

River crossings could be a major hazard. In early times they were fords, not bridges, as is shown by the number of names ending in 'ford' on the old London–Chester road through the county—Weeford, Meaford, Strongford, Hanford. When bridges were eventually built they were not always a great improvement. The most notable bridge in the county was that at Burton, over a quarter of a mile long and mentioned soon after 1100. Its upkeep was the responsibility of the monks of Burton, but many charitable gifts were made towards its maintenance. Yet this important bridge remained barely wide enough for one carriage right up until its replacement in the 1860s. As late as 1662 Darlaston bridge, near Stone, although carrying an important highway across the Trent, was still wide enough only for horses; carriages had to ford the river, at considerable risk in times of flood. The county court of Quarter Sessions then decided that it should be rebuilt as a bridge for 'carts and wagons to pass over' and ordered £200 to be levied on the county for the purpose.

By a law of 1555 the upkeep of roads was made the responsibility of the parishes through which they passed. This was not only unfair; it was also inefficient, with the result that by the 18th century the road system was inadequate for the rapidly increasing needs of the time. Already in the 1680s Robert Plot in his *Natural History of Staffordshire* observed that while the roads of the county were on the whole good, those in the industrial area around Wednesbury, Sedgley and Dudley were 'uncessantly [*sic*] worn with the carriage of coal'. In 1728 a former postmaster at Stone stated that the main road there was 'worn deep with heavy carriages' and that the expenditure of large sums and the constant performance of the required parish work were not enough to keep the road in repair; furthermore, between Canwell and Darlaston it ran through 'several hollow ways which render such parts of the road impassable when any quantity of snow falls'.

The solution adopted was the system of turnpike trusts—groups of local trustees responsible for given stretches of road and levying tolls for the upkeep of those stretches on the people who used them. The first trust in England was established in 1663 on part of the Great North Road. The first in Staffordshire was set up by Act of Parliament in 1714 to cover the London–Carlisle road from Darlaston to the county boundary beyond Talke.

It was another 12 years before the establishment of the next Staffordshire turnpike trust, that concerned with the Birmingham–Wednesbury road. In 1729 the whole Staffordshire section of the

*Milepost of 1834 on the
Leek-Ashbourne road*

Chester road via Lichfield was turnpiked, along with the Lichfield–Burton road. The alternative Chester route via Brownhills and Watling Street was turnpiked in 1760. In 1749 three roads radiating from Walsall were turnpiked in order that 'the price of the carriage of goods might be reduced' and the needs of local traders thereby served. The turnpiking of the roads around Bilston in 1766 was another important development for the growing industrial area in the south of the county. In the early 19th century the Bilston trust acquired new importance when one of its roads became part of the official mail-coach route from London to Holyhead, which ran through West Bromwich, ednesbury, Bilston, Wolverhampton, and Tettenhall.

In the north the development of the Potteries was dependent on the improvement of the roads in the area. That began with the turnpiking of the road from Uttoxeter to Newcastle in 1759 through the south of the district. The extension of the system throughout the Potteries during the next few years was the work of Josiah Wedgwood and his associates, despite strong opposition from the vested interests of Newcastle, determined to preserve the town's monopoly as the ancient centre of communications in the area. The second half of the century also saw the turnpiking of the roads over the difficult high ground in the north-east of the county. One of the most important was the Macclesfield–Leek–Ashbourne road, turnpiked in 1762. It was along this road that the Young Pretender had marched to Derby in 1745, and it now provided the shortest route for coaches between London and Manchester. Most of the Staffordshire turnpiking was carried out before 1800, but improvements did not stop there. As late as the 1840s a completely new turnpike road was built to connect Stoke with Leek via Abbey Hulton and Endon.

The turnpikes ushered in the coaching era. Staffordshire was served by long-distance coaches to London, Birmingham, and Bristol in the south, and Holyhead, Chester, Liverpool and Manchester in the north, with names such as the *Bang-up, Erin-go-bragh, Red Rover, Beehive* and *Royal Dart.* No fewer than 29 coaches passed through Newcastle daily in November 1830. Surviving examples of coaching inns are the *George* at Lichfield, and the *Crown* at Stone; the *Castle* at Newcastle has been converted into a supermarket, but much of its original façade has been preserved.

The turnpike trusts varied greatly in efficiency and were also too limited in scope. A more centralised and effective system of highway administration did not come until the late 19th century in Staffordshire, which resisted the general trend. In the meantime the men of the Industrial Revolution developed an alternative means of transporting their goods and materials—waterways.

94

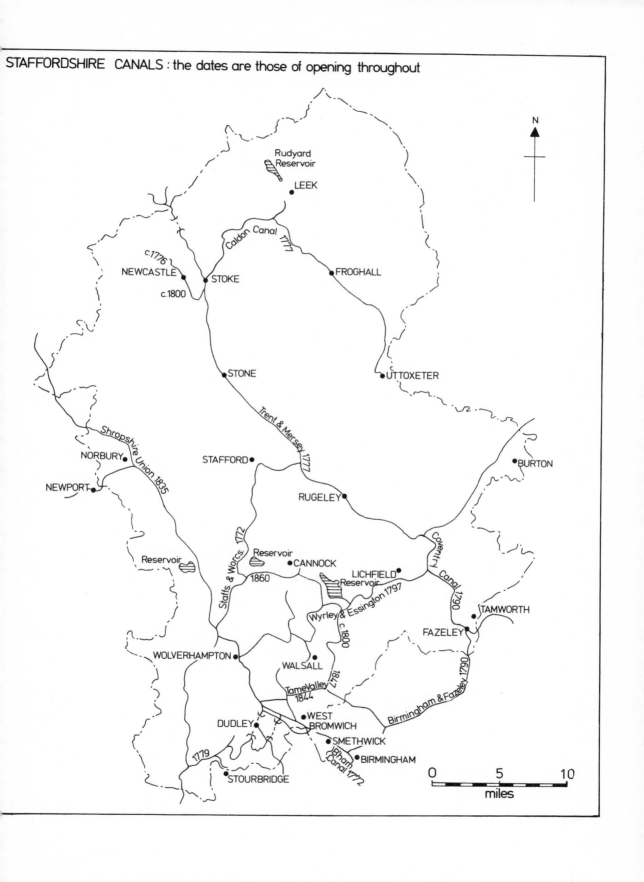

STAFFORDSHIRE CANALS : the dates are those of opening throughout

N

Rudyard
Reservoir

LEEK

Caldon Canal 1777

c.1776
NEWCASTLE
STOKE
c.1800
FROGHALL

STONE

UTTOXETER

Shropshire Union 1835

NORBURY
STAFFORD
BURTON

NEWPORT
RUGELEY

Staffs. & Worcs. 1772

Reservoir
Reservoir
CANNOCK
1860
LICHFIELD
Reservoir
Coventry Canal 1790

Wyrley & Essington 1797

Wyrley & Essington c.1800
TAMWORTH

FAZELEY
WOLVERHAMPTON
WALSALL
1847

Tame Valley
1844
Birmingham & Fazeley 1790

DUDLEY
WEST
BROMWICH
SMETHWICK
1779
BIRMINGHAM
Bir'ham
Canal 1772
0        5        10
STOURBRIDGE
miles

*James Brindley*

Staffordshire is an inland county and has no navigable rivers. At first there were schemes to improve the rivers. Under an Act of 1662 an attempt was made to render the Stour navigable from Stourbridge to Stourport through the south-west corner of Staffordshire. Part of the work involved the cutting of a trench close to the river through the north-west of Kinver parish; the trench, though now dry, is still clearly visible for most of its length. Under an Act of 1699 the Trent was improved downstream from Burton, and the main practical result seems to have been the opening of the way to Hull and the Baltic for the Burton brewers. In 1717 there was an unsuccessful attempt to link the Trent and the Severn by a mixture of river improvement and canal building in south-west Staffordshire.

The first canal to be started in the county was the Trent and Mersey —also known as the Grand Trunk—linking the Mersey and the Humber via the Trent. It was the work of James Brindley, the pioneering genius of inland waterways. The first sod was cut near Burslem in 1766 by Josiah Wedgwood; shortly after work had begun on the canal, he built his new factory at Etruria beside it, the first of many potteries to be sited along the canal. It took 11 years to finish the canal, mainly because of the time required to construct Harecastle tunnel, nearly 1¾ miles long, through the high ground north of the Potteries. As there was no towpath underground until Thomas Telford built a second tunnel in the 1820s, boats had to be legged through by the boatmen.

The Trent and Mersey linked Staffordshire with Liverpool in the north-west and Hull in the north-east. An outlet to Bristol and the south-west was provided by Brindley's Staffordshire and Worcestershire Canal built in 1766–72, running from the Trent and Mersey at Great Haywood, near Stafford, to the Severn at Stourport in Worcestershire. Finally the county was linked with London and the south-east by means of a canal completed in 1790 from the Trent and Mersey at Fradley, north of Lichfield, to Coventry, whence another canal ran to the Thames at Oxford. Staffordshire thus became the hub of the national canal system as befitted its midland situation.

Several other canals were built to link various regions with the main system or to provide short cuts. The first branch canal in England was the Birmingham Canal constructed by Brindley in 1768–72 to provide an outlet for the increasingly important industries of the Black Country. It runs from Birmingham via Smethwick, Tipton, Coseley, Bilston, and Wolverhampton to join the Staffordshire and Worcestershire at Aldersley north-west of Wolverhampton. Just over 50 years after its opening it was straightened and improved by Telford, who cut seven miles out of its length and reduced the number of locks

44. The Elizabethan shire hall, Stafford, from the west, c.1680. (*Plot*, Staffordshire.)

45. The market place, Stafford, from the north, showing the shire hall of 1798 on the left, the guild hall of 1854 on the right, and a Russian cannon captured during the Crimean War. Lithograph by E.H. Buckler, published in 1859. (*William Salt Library.*)

46.  Walsall from the north-west, about 1800. (*S. Shaw*, The History and Antiquities of Staffordshire, *ii, 1801.*)

47.  High Street, Newcastle under Lyme, from the south-east in 1839. (*I. Cottrill*, Police Directory of Newcastle-under-Lyme, *1839; copy in William Salt Library.* )

from thirty to twenty-four. His work included the cast-iron Galton bridge of 1829 carrying Roebuck Lane, the road between West Bromwich and Smethwick, over a new cutting 70 feet deep. With its span of 154 feet it was the longest canal bridge in the world; it was made at the Horseley ironworks in Tipton. The last canals date from the later 1850s. In 1858 the Netherton tunnel was opened from the Birmingham Canal to the Dudley Canal, a short cut serving the mines of the Stour valley; the last canal tunnel to be built in England, it was lit by gas and had two towpaths. To serve the growing Cannock Chase coalfield a canal was opened to Churchbridge in 1860 and to Hednesford in 1863.

*The northern end of the Harecastle tunnels*

By then both turnpikes and canals were facing severe competition from a quicker and cheaper means of transport—the railway. This originated largely as a means of transporting goods by horse-drawn wagons to and from canal wharves. In 1777 the Caldon Low limestone quarries in the north-east were linked with the Caldon Canal at Froghall by a tramway. In 1805 another tramway was opened from Radford wharf on the Staffordshire and Worcestershire Canal south-east of Stafford to a terminus by Green bridge in the town, a distance of 1½ miles. In 1829 a 3½-mile railway was opened to connect the earl of Dudley's coal pits at Shut End in Kingswinford with the Staffordshire and Worcestershire Canal at Ashwood.

The first railway of national importance was also the first of importance in Staffordshire. The Grand Junction Railway linking Birmingham with Merseyside was built under an Act of 1834 and opened in 1837, running through the Black Country and Stafford. In 1838 it was extended south to the Birmingham–London line. A more direct route to London from the North was provided by the Trent Valley Railway opened from Stafford to Rugby in 1847, avoiding Birmingham. A line from Birmingham to Tamworth, Burton and Derby was completed in 1842 and gave a new boost to the Burton brewing industry. Railway development often involved fierce struggles between rival companies, such as the fight between the London and North-Western Railway and the Great Western Railway for the Black Country, which in the 1850s resulted in two separate but parallel systems between Birmingham and Wolverhampton.

As with the canals earlier, the creation of the national system of railways was followed by the construction of more local lines. In 1848-9 the North Staffordshire Railway ('the Knotty') was opened from Colwich (on the London line) to Macclesfield (on the Manchester line) via the Potteries, bringing the North Staffordshire industrial area into the national system; a local loop line through the Potteries was completed in the 1870s. The Cannock Chase coalfield was

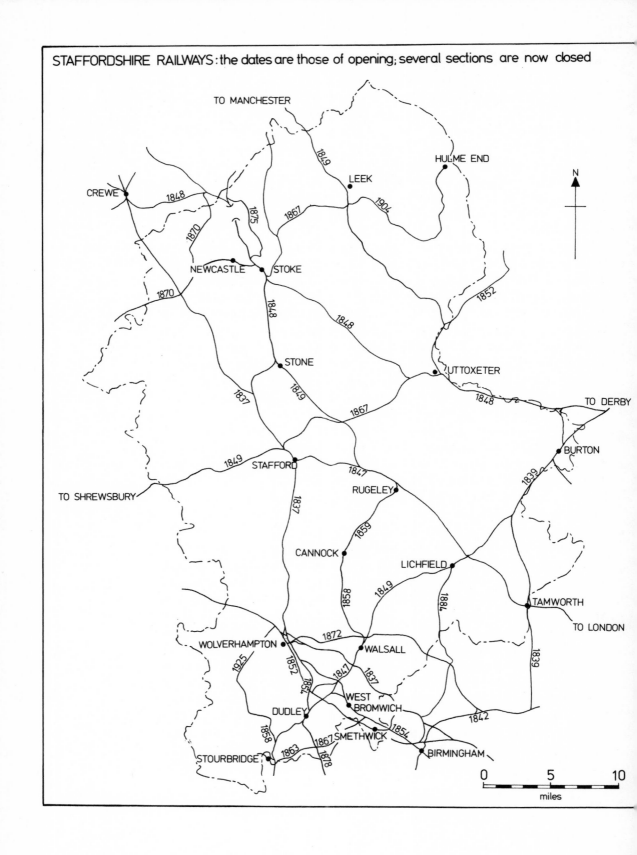

STAFFORDSHIRE RAILWAYS: the dates are those of opening; several sections are now closed

TO MANCHESTER

HULME END
LEEK

CREWE
1848

1849
1875
1867
1904

1870
NEWCASTLE   STOKE
1852

1870
1848
1848

STONE
UTTOXETER

1837
1849
1867
1848
TO DERBY

TO SHREWSBURY
1849
STAFFORD
1847
RUGELEY
BURTON
1839

1837
1859

CANNOCK
LICHFIELD

1858
1849
1884
TAMWORTH
TO LONDON

1925
1872
WALSALL
1839

WOLVERHAMPTON
1852
1847
1837

WEST BROMWICH
DUDLEY
1854
1842

1858
1867
SMETHWICK
1863
1878
BIRMINGHAM
STOURBRIDGE

N

0        5        10
miles

penetrated in the late 1850s by a branch of the South Staffordshire Railway. It ran from Walsall to Cannock and was continued by the Cannock Mineral line from Cannock to the London line at Rugeley. As late as 1925 the Wolverhampton and Kingswinford Railway was opened through the south-west of the county; it was begun in 1913, but work was delayed by the First World War.

The railways were not only cheaper and quicker for freight, and so a threat the canals; they were also better for passengers and so spelled the sudden end of the coaching age and the eventual end of the turnpikes. Newcastle's 29 coaches of 1830 had dwindled to three by 1839. However, an omnibus then ran from the *King's Head* in Newcastle to the Grand Junction line at Whitmore, five miles away. The railways, in fact, stimulated a new, more local form of road transport which brought passengers 'to the rails' from the inns and outlying parts. With the opening of the railway through Stafford in 1837 the *Staffordshire Advertiser* reported the introduction of 'a handsome omnibus' between the *Swan* and the new station: 'the driver and the guard (a boy) are habited in scarlet uniform, and the appearance of the whole set-out is very respectable'. The development of the towns meant a further increase in such local transport. Trams were introduced in the Potteries in 1862, and were themselves displaced by motor buses some 60 years later.

The great development in communications in the 20th century has been air travel. In the 1930s Walsall, Wolverhampton and Stoke on Trent opened municipal airports, although none survives. During the Second World War several airfields were in use in the county. That at Halfpenny Green in Bobbington in the south-west, which continues to be used for civilian flying, was in 1972 the scene of an accident in which Prince William of Gloucester was killed.

In the later 20th century the internal combustion engine has to some extent brought the story full circle. Railway competition led to the decline of roads and canals from the later 19th century. In the 1980s the canal network is still largely intact, but it is pleasure cruising and not commercial traffic that is important. The railways have suffered from the competition of road traffic, and most local lines have been closed. The main lines have been electrified, and some of their stations rebuilt; at Stafford, for example, in 1962 a new station replaced one of 1862. Meanwhile the roads themselves have entered a new era. Many have been widened to take extra traffic. Thus the road between Wolverhampton and Penkridge was made into a dual carriageway in the 1930s, crossing Watling Street at Gailey where the roundabout dates from 1937. Many are now completely new, built as by-passes to reduce congestion in towns and villages. An early example is

*Stafford station in 1844*

Birmingham New Road between Wolverhampton and Birmingham, built in the mid 1920s under a scheme to relieve unemployment; 9¾ miles long, it serves as a by-pass for several Black Country towns. The motorways of the 1960s and 1970s have made Staffordshire once more the centre of a communications system. In a large triangular intersection north of West Bromwich, completed in 1970, the M5 from the south-west of England joins the M6 running from the north-west to the M1 and London.

*The Crown Hotel, Stone, about 1800*

# XIII  The Civilised Social Life

By the mid 19th century Staffordshire has been transformed into a great industrial county. Before the Industrial Revolution its towns were mainly small market towns. In 1086 Domesday Book recorded Stafford, Tutbury and Tamworth as boroughs. Lichfield was described as 'a small village' about 1125, but about the middle of the century a town appears to have been laid out by the bishops south of the cathedral. Also about then a new town grew up in the shadow of the new castle of Newcastle under Lyme. At Burton the monks laid out a town at the abbey's gate at the end of the century. Leek, too, has the appearance of a planned medieval town, perhaps dating from the same period. Walsall secured borough status in the course of the 13th century. Wolverhampton was granted a Wednesday market and an annual eight-day fair by royal charter in 1258, although it had a market by 1203; the town was prospering on the wool and cloth trade by about 1400. Lichfield, Stone and Newcastle, situated on a busy road, benefited from coaching traffic in the 18th century.

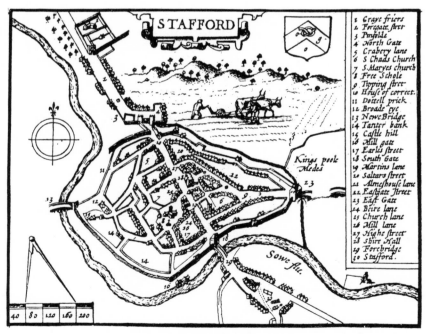

*John Speed's plan of Stafford (1610)*

Between 1801 and 1901 the population of Staffordshire increased by almost a million from 242,693 to 1,234,533, the fourth largest of any English county. Among the older towns Wolverhampton rose from 12,565 inhabitants to 94,187, and Walsall from 10,399 to 87,464. Otherwise the increase in the older towns was less rapid; Stafford, for example, rose from 3,898 to 14,060, and Newcastle from 4,604 to 19,147. Elsewhere villages and scattered settlements became important towns. West Bromwich rose from 5,687 inhabitants to 65,114, Cannock from 1,359 to 23,974, and Burslem from 6,578 to 40,234. Most dramatic of all was Smethwick, which leapt from 1,097 to 54,539.

In 1781 John Wesley marvelled at the changing landscape of the Potteries:

> How is the whole face of this country changed in about 20 years. Since the potteries were introduced, inhabitants have continually flowed in from every side. Hence the wilderness is literally become a fruitful field: houses, villages, towns have sprung up.

That picture is too rosy, at any rate for the 19th century. It was then that the Black Country acquired its name—'black by day, red by night', wrote an American in the 1860s; Arnold Bennett compared the Potteries to Dante's Inferno. An official report published in 1843 described the haphazard growth of Wolverhampton:

> In process of time, as the inhabitants increased in number, small rooms were raised over [the] workshops, and hovels also built wherever room could be found, and tenanted, first perhaps as workshops, and gradually by families also. By these means the rapidly increasing population were lodged from year to year, while the circumference of the town remained almost the same for a long time, owing to the difficulty of obtaining land to build upon, as it was all private property or belonged to the church. As soon as land was obtained, Stafford Street and Walsall Street were built for the working classes, two of the longest and most disgraceful streets in the town . . . In one of the hovels of Stafford Street it appeared that a man, his wife and a child, and a donkey all slept together . . . None of these houses and hovels in courts and alleys have any underground drainage, and very few of them have any privies . . . There is often a common dunghill at one end or in one corner, where everything is cast; but more generally there is nothing but the gutter and the passage into the street.

*The arms of Stafford borough used from the 17th century until 1974*

In 1849 Burslem's inhabitants were stated to be living 'upon a volcano of epidemics', while Hanley was 'surrounded by a moat filled with decomposing filth'. An assize judge staying in Stafford in 1870 described it as 'the most stinking town I was ever in in my life', noting in particular the sewage which flowed down open channels in the main streets. The state of Stafford's streets was made worse by their use

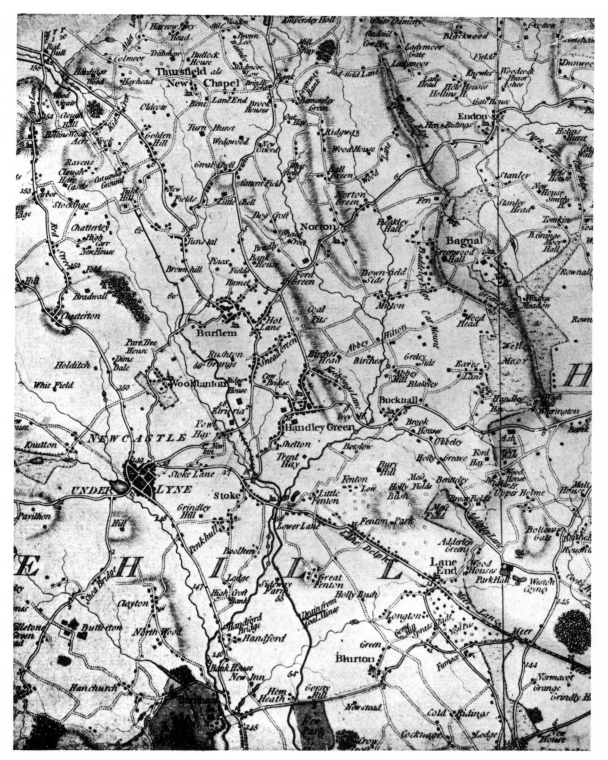

Newcastle under Lyme and the Potteries area from W. Yates' *A Map of the County of Stafford*, 1775.

for cattle markets and fairs, and there were complaints about 'the disgusting filth and indecent scenes' which resulted. The evils were underlined by the cholera outbreaks of 1832 and 1848–9. In the first Bilston suffered particularly, with 743 deaths out of a population of some 15,000; in the second 2,683 people died in the county out of a population of some 600,000.

Such evils were matched by bad working conditions, sweated labour and the extensive employment of women and children. In the Staffordshire mines conditions were not so bad as in many others for no women worked below ground; but numbers of them were employed at the pit-head and in loading and unloading canal boats. Of the children in the Wolverhampton area about 1840 it was said that 'their minds were as stunted as their bodies, their moral feelings stagnant as the nutritive processes whereby they should have been built up towards maturity'. Arnold Bennett's description in *Clayhanger* of the depravity of the potbanks in the earlier 19th century and the misery of the small boys employed there was based on the memories of Charles Shaw, who, born in Tunstall in 1832, had experienced them himself. Some children started work with a 72-hour week at the age of five. As late as 1862 twenty-six of the more enlightened pottery manufacturers urged the Home Secretary to take legislative action to protect children in the potworks, stating that most of them were taken from school before they were 10, with the result that they were ignorant, stunted and consumptive. The potters were also exposed to special health dangers—lead poisoning and 'potter's rot', a disease caused by breathing in flint dust; neither was seriously faced until the end of the 19th century. Yet trade unionism was slow to take root, especially among the potters.

At the same time, what one historian has described as 'the organisation of a civilised social life' gradually took place. The existing organs of manor, parish and borough were supplemented and eventually replaced. Boards of improvement commissioners were set up by Act of Parliament to pave, light, watch, cleanse and regulate towns—as at Wolverhampton in 1777, Burton upon Trent in 1779, Lichfield in 1806, Newcastle under Lyme in 1819, Walsall in 1824, Burslem and Leek in 1825, and Stafford in 1830. At Newcastle the commissioners' powers passed to the borough as reformed under the Municipal Corporations Act of 1835, but at Stafford the powers were not transferred until 1875. At Burslem the commissioners were superseded in 1850 by a board of health, itself replaced by a new borough in 1878. In 1889, under the Local Government Act of 1888, the new county council took over the administrative powers exercised for centuries by the county justices, while four county boroughs were created—

*The arms of the county borough, later city, of Stoke on Trent granted in 1908*

104

48. Penkhull Square (built c.1800). (*National Monuments Record.*)

Nineteenth-century workers' houses in the Potteries

49. (*left*) Piccadilly Street, Tunstall (1821). (*Photograph by Margaret Tomlinson.*)
50. (*below left*) Granville Street, Cobridge (1853). (*Photograph by Margaret Tomlinson; Victoria History of the Counties of England.*)
51. Beresford Street, Hanley (1878). (*Photograph by Margaret Tomlinson; Victoria History of the Counties of England.*)

The Wolverhampton Orphan Asylum about 1900. The School was renamed the Royal Orphanage of Wolverhampton in 1900 and the Royal Wolverhampton School in 1946. (*Wolverhampton Central Library*.)

52. (*above*) The girls' department.
53. (*below*) The boys' department.

Hanley, Walsall, West Bromwich, and Wolverhampton. Burton was added to the county boroughs in 1901 and Smethwick in 1906. In 1910 the six Potteries towns of Tunstall, Burslem, Hanley, Stoke upon Trent, Fenton, and Longton amalgamated as the county borough of Stoke on Trent; it became a city in 1925.

Another important new authority, created under the Act of 1834 reforming the poor law, was the poor-law union, usually covering several parishes and symbolised by the workhouse. The Stoke upon Trent union formed in 1836 retained the Stoke parish workhouse built on the Newcastle road three years before, enlarging it to meet new requirements; its buildings have been incorporated in the City General Hospital. The Wolstanton and Burslem union, on the other hand, built a new workhouse in the late 1830s at Chell, near Tunstall; it cost £6,200 and had accommodation for four hundred. The shame and horror felt by a family sent there soon afterwards were vividly recorded by Charles Shaw, whose description was again used by Bennett in *Clayhanger.*

It was, however, private enterprise which initially attempted to deal with the social problems for whose creation it was largely responsible. In the field of health the Staffordshire General Infirmary was established at Stafford by subscribers in 1766; in 1818 the county justices, the trustees of the infirmary, and subscribers opened the Staffordshire General Lunatic Asylum in the town. In the Potteries a 'house of recovery' for the poor, supported by voluntary contributions, was built in Etruria Vale in 1804; it was the predecessor of the North Staffordshire Infirmary opened nearby in 1819 and moved to Hartshill in 1869. A dispensary supported by subscribers was opened at Wolverhampton in 1825, the predecessor of the South Staffordshire General Hospital opened there in 1848.

A pure water supply is another essential of public health. In 1820 John Smith started a waterworks at Ivy House in Hanley and supplied Hanley, Shelton and Burslem; but the quality was poor and the supply inadequate. The Potteries Waterworks Co. was incorporated in 1847, with its first works at Wall Grange, south of Leek. Wolverhampton was supplied by the Wolverhampton Waterworks Co. which was incorporated in 1845 and opened its first works at Tettenhall two years later. A wider area of the south was supplied by the South Staffordshire Waterworks Co. incorporated in 1853; its first works was opened at Lichfield in 1858, using the two pools by the cathedral as reservoirs. The company's reservoir at Blithfield opened in 1953 is a notable feature of Staffordshire landscape; over two miles long, it covers 790 acres of former park and farming land, and is crossed by a viaduct half a mile long carrying the Rugeley–Abbots Bromley road.

*Waterworks at the Bratch, Wombourne, built by Bilston urban district council in the mid-1890s*

SOME TYPICAL

19th – CENTURY PLANS

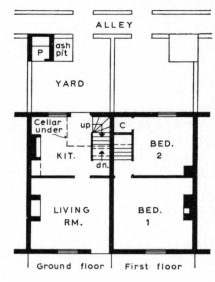

Privies in Communal Yard

PENKHULL SQUARE

STOKE *c.*1800

PICCADILLY STREET

TUNSTALL 1821

```
0    5   10        20        30
□□□□ □□□ □□  □  □  □  □
scale of feet
```

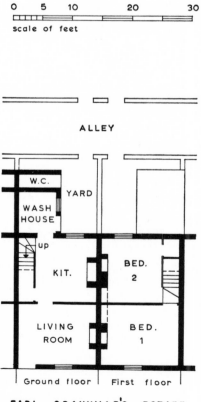

EARL GRANVILLE'S ESTATE

(SMALLER TYPE) COBRIDGE 1853

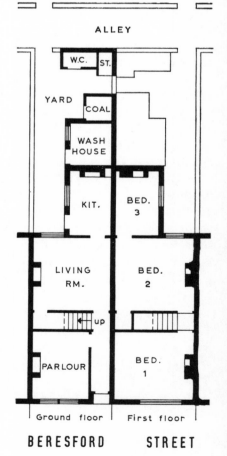

BERESFORD STREET

HANLEY 1878

*Workers' terraced housing in the Potteries*

As early as the 1760s Josiah Wedgwood had provided at Etruria a standard of housing for his workers which was advanced for its day, terraces of four-roomed cottages with a well and pump for every few dwellings, and communal bakehouses. At Rocester Richard Arkwright built brick terraces for the workers at the cotton mill which he opened in the early 1780s, while at Fazeley Robert Peel built model houses for the workers at the cotton mill opened about 1790, probably the first fireproof houses in the country. Self-help in house building was active in the Potteries by 1807 when the Burslem United and Amicable Building Society was offering three grades of housing, all with their own yards and land for gardens. In 1821 Tunstall Building Society, founded in 1816 with many working potters as members, built two terraces west of the town centre, each of 20 houses; all had their own privy and ashpit. A striking advance was made by Earl Granville in the mid 1850s when he built a large estate at Cobridge for his workers; all the houses had a wash-house and water-closet, most had front gardens, some had entrance halls and a third bedroom. An early example of a middle-class estate is The Villas, near Boothen in Stoke upon Trent; dating from the mid 19th century, it consists of stucco houses in an Italianate style, detached and in pairs. In Stafford Rowley Park began to be laid out in the 1860s with 'suburban residences of a superior class' over part of the grounds of Rowley Hall.

*Stafford grammar school in 1837*

Advances in education continued to be the work of the churches and of private philanthropy as for centuries past. Some older towns had grammar schools which dated from before the Reformation. At Stafford in 1380 there was mention of 'Thomas the schoolmaster' and also of 'Catherine the schoolmistress'; a grammar school was attached to St Mary's church by about 1500, probably the same school as that where the bishop was supporting three poor boys in 1473. In the early 17th century the rector of Stoke upon Trent, then still a rural area, maintained a school at Stoke where 40 boys were taught reading, writing and the catechism, and another at Shelton where girls were taught to read, spin, knit, and sew. At West Bromwich there was a school by 1686, apparently a private academy, and less than a century later there were several private schools and schools for the poor. In addition a Sunday school was opened in 1786 by the Presbyterian minister, George Osborne, who was a pioneer of the Sunday school movement; in 1788 the Anglicans followed suit at the parish church. West Bromwich grew rapidly in the early 19th century; two Church of England schools were duly opened for boys and for girls in 1811, while the Wesleyan Methodists started a school in 1826 and the Roman Catholics another in 1834. Employers also opened schools for their workers. By 1842 the Kenricks were running one at their Summit Foundry in West Bromwich. In 1845-6 the Chances started one at their glassworks in Smethwick, including a Sunday school and an evening school for older boys. Earl Granville's Cobridge estate included a school, opened in 1854. The cholera epidemic of 1849 inspired John Lee, a Wolverhampton lock and key manufacturer, to found the Wolverhampton Orphan Asylum (now the Royal Wolverhampton School) in 1850.

These were some of the many improvements which have produced the late 20th-century scene. While the main urban areas are still concentrated in the north and south of the county, the Black Country is no longer black, and clean air has come to the Potteries with the disappearance of the familiar bottle ovens as firms changed to gas and electric firing. Wedgwoods went further. Just as Josiah moved from Burslem to open country at Etruria in the 1760s, so in the late 1930s the firm built an electric-fired works in parklands at Barlaston, a few miles to the south, and then gradually abandoned the Etruria works.

The historic pottery at Etruria was eventually demolished, but belatedly the remains of the industrial past have become an object of conservation. The Black Country museum, near Dudley, recreates the local scene, and includes a village, complete with chapel and chainmaker's workshop, and the re-opened Dudley canal tunnel 1¾ miles long and dating from the 1790s. Near Tunstall the former Chatterley-Whitfield colliery has been turned into a mining museum which offers tours 700 feet below ground. In the centre of Longton the mid 19th-century Gladstone potworks was opened in 1975 as a working pottery museum. It preserves a fine group of bottle ovens, but the smokey scene has to be left to the imagination.

*Stafford Union workhouse in 1843.*

# Bibliography

| | |
|---|---|
| N.S.J.F.S. | *North Staffordshire Journal of Field Studies.* |
| S.H.C. | Staffordshire Record Society (formerly William Salt Archaeological Society), *Collections for a History of Staffordshire* (also called *Staffordshire Historical Collections*). |
| T.N.S.F.C. | *Transactions of the North Staffordshire Field Club.* |
| T.S.S.A.H.S. | *Transactions of the South Staffordshire Archaeological and Historical Society* (formerly *Transactions of the Lichfield and South Staffordshire Archaeological and and Historical Society*). |
| V.C.H. Staffs. | *Victoria County History of Staffordshire.* |

## General

S. Erdeswick, *A Survey of Staffordshire*, ed. T. Harwood (1844); M. W. Greenslade, *The Staffordshire Historians* (*S.H.C.*, 4th ser. xi); P. Murray and R. Frost, *Victorian and Edwardian Staffordshire from old photographs* (1977); D. M. Palliser, *The Staffordshire Landscape* (1976); N. Pevsner, *Staffordshire* (1974); W. Pitt, *A Topographical History of Staffordshire* (1817); R. Plot, *The Natural History of Staffordshire* (1686); J. Raven, *The Folklore of Staffordshire* (1978); S. Shaw, *The History and Antiquities of Staffordshire* (2 vols., 1798, 1801; reprinted 1976); H. Thorold, *Staffordshire* (1978); W. White, *History, Gazetteer, and Directory of Staffordshire* (edns. of 1834 and 1851).

## Chapter I (The Setting)

*V.C.H. Staffs.*, i, article on 'Geology'; S. H. Beaver and B. J. Turton, *The Potteries*, (1979); R. Milward and A. Robinson, *The West Midlands* (1971); V. Skipp, *The Centre of England* (1979); E. J. D. Warrilow, *Arnold Bennett and Stoke-on-Trent* (1966).

## Chapter II (Prehistoric and Roman Times).

*V.C.H. Staffs.*, i, articles on 'Early Man', 'Romano-British Staffordshire'; J. M. T. Charlton, 'Excavations at the Roman Site at Holditch', *N.S.J.F.S.*, i; G. Webster, 'Excavations at the Roman Site at Rocester, Staffordshire, 1961', *N.S.J.F.S.*, ii; E. W. Ball, 'A Rectangular Earthwork at Chesterton, Staffordshire', *N.S.J.F.S.*, iv; A. J. H. Gunstone, 'An Archaeological Gazetteer of Staffordshire, Part 1: chance finds and sites, excluding barrows and their contents', *N.S.J.F.S.*, iv; 'Part 2: The Barrows', *N.S.J.F.S.*, v; F. H. Goodyear, 'The Roman Fort at Chesterton, Newcastle-under-Lyme: Report of the Excavations of 1969–71', *N.S.J.F.S.*, xvi; J. Gould, 'Excavations at Wall (Staffordshire), 1964–6 on the site of the Roman forts', *T.S.S.A.H.S.*, viii; A. A. Round, A. Ross, M. Henig, 'Eleventh Report of Excavations at

Wall, Staffs.', *T.S.S.A.H.S.*, xxi; M. A. Hodder, 'The Prehistory of the Lichfield Area', *T.S.S.A.H.S.*, xxiii; A. A. Round, 'Excavations at Wall (Staffordshire), 1968-72, on the site of the Roman Forts (Wall Excavations Report No. 12)', *T.S.S.A.H.S.*, xxiii; G. Webster, *The Cornivii* (1975).

### Chapter III (The Anglo-Saxon Period)

*V.C.H. Staffs.*, i, articles on 'Anglo-Saxon Remains', 'Political History'; S. Losco-Bradley, 'Catholme', *Current Archaeology*, lix; P. Rahtz and K. Sheridan, 'Fifth Report of Excavations at Tamworth, Staffs., 1971', *T.S.S.A.H.S.*, xiii; D. Hooke, *The Landscape of Anglo-Saxon Staffordshire: The Charter Evidence* (1983).

### Chapter IV (The Norman Conquest)

*V.C.H. Staffs.*, ii, article on 'Forests'; iv, introduction to and text of the Staffordshire section of Domesday Book; *Domesday Book, Staffordshire* (1976), ed. J. Morris.

### Chapter V (County Families and their Houses)

*V.C.H. Staffs.*, v, articles on 'Brewood', 'Castle Church'; xvii, article on 'West Bromwich'; G. Wrottesley, 'The Giffard family from the Conquest to the present time', *S.H.C.*, new ser. v; G. Wrottesley, 'The History of the Bagot Family', *S.H.C.*, new ser. xi; D. Palliser, 'Staffordshire Castles: a provisional list', *Staffordshire Archaeology*, i; *Stafford Castle* (Staffordshire County Council Local History Source Book, L. 2); *Stafford Castle, Third Interim Report*, (1981) (Stafford Borough Council); R. Somerville, *Guide to Tutbury Castle, Staffordshire* (1978); R. A. Meeson, 'Tenth Tamworth Excavation Report, 1977: The Norman bailey defences of the castle', *T.S.S.A.H.S.*, xx; J. Cornforth, 'Trentham, Staffordshire', *Country Life*, Jan.–Feb. 1968; S. R. Gammon, *Statesman and Schemer: William, First Lord Paget, Tudor Minister* (1973); J. Godwin, *Beaudesert and the Pagets* (Staffordshire County Library, 1982); J. M. Kolbert, *The Sneyds, Squires of Keele* (University of Keele, 1976); C. Rawcliffe, *The Staffords, Earls of Stafford and Dukes of Buckingham* (1978); *Shugborough, Staffordshire* (Staffordshire County Council and National Trust, n.d.); D. Stuart, *Dear Duchess* (1982); H. Wood, *Borough by Prescription* (Tamworth Corporation, 1958).

### Chapter VI (Churches and Monasteries)

*V.C.H. Staffs.*, ii, articles on 'The Medieval Church', 'The Church of England since the Reformation', 'Religious Houses' (including 'Lichfield Cathedral'), iv, article on 'Gnosall'; v, article on 'Penkridge'; vol. vi, article on 'Stafford': *The Cartulary of Tutbury Priory*, ed. A. Saltman (*S.H.C.*, 4th ser., iv); *Bishop Geoffrey Blythe's Visitation, c. 1515-1525*, ed. P. Heath (*S.H.C.*, 4th ser., vii); F. A. Hibbert, *The Dissolution of the Monasteries, as illustrated by the suppression of the religious houses of Staffordshire* (1910); *Bede's Ecclesiastical History of the English People*, ed. B. Colgrave and R. A. B. Mynors (1969), from which the quotation on p. 45 is taken.

### Chapter VII (Reformers and Recusants)

*V.C.H. Staffs.*, iii, articles on 'The Church of England since the Reformation', 'Roman Catholicism', 'Protestant Nonconformity'; W. N. Landor, *Staffordshire Incumbents and Parochial Records (1530-1680)* (*S.H.C.*, 1915); *The*

*Registrations of Dissenting Chapels and Meeting Houses in Staffordshire,
1689-1852*, ed. B. Donaldson (*S.H.C.*, 4th ser. iii); *Roman Catholicism in
Elizabethan and Jacobean Staffordshire*, ed. A. G. Petti (*S.H.C.*, 4th ser. ix);
*Staffordshire Catholic History*, 1961 to date (The Journal of the Staffordshire Catholic History Society); A. G. Matthews, *The Congregational Churches
of Staffordshire* (n.d., but preface 1924).

## Chapter VIII (The Civil War and Commonwealth Period)

R. M. Kidson, 'The Gentry of Staffordshire, 1662-1663' and 'Staffordshire Parlia-
mentarians in the Civil War, 1662', *S.H.C.*, 4th ser. ii; *The Committee at
Stafford, 1643-45*, ed. D. H. Pennington and I. A. Roots (*S.H.C.*, 4th ser. i);
G. Wrottesley, 'Staffordshire during the Civil War', *T.N.S.F.C.*, xlv; D. A.
Johnson and D. G. Vaisey, *Staffordshire and the Great Rebellion* (Stafford-
shire County Council, 1964); R. E. Sherwood, *Civil Strife in the Midlands*
(1974); C. H. Simpkinson, *The Life of Thomas Harrison* (1905); *The Civil
War In Staffordshire: the Battle of Hopton Heath* (Staffordshire County
Council, 1967).

## Chapter IX (Elections and Party Politics)

*V.C.H. Staffs.*, vi, viii, xvii, sections on 'Parliamentary Representation'; J. C. Wedgwood, 'Staffordshire Parliamentary History', *S.H.C.*, 1917-18, 1920 and 1922,
1933 (i); S. M. Hardy and R. C. Baily, 'The Downfall of the Gower interest in
the Staffordshire Boroughs', *S.H.C.*, 1950 and 1951; A. J. Kettle, 'The Struggle
for the Lichfield Interest', *S.H.C.*, 4th ser. vi; E. Richards, 'The Social and
Electoral Influence of the Trentham Interest, 1800-1860', *Midland History*,
iii; D. Rolf, 'Labour and Politics in the West Midlands between the Wars',
*N.S.J.F.S.*, xviii; D. G. Stuart, 'Castle and Manor: parliamentary patronage
in the borough of Tamworth in the mid eighteenth century', *T.S.S.A.H.S.*,
ix; G. B. Kent, 'The Beginnings of Party Political Organization in Staffordshire, 1832-41', *N.S.J.F.S.*, i; F. Burchill and R. Ross, *A History of the
Potters' Union* (1977); R. Fyson, 'The Crisis of 1842: Chartism, the Colliers'
Strike and the Outbreak in the Potteries', in *The Chartist Experience* (1982),
ed. J. Epstein and D. Thompson; D. Stuart, *County Borough: the History of
Burton upon Trent, 1901-1974, Part 1, Edwardian Burton*, ch. 13; *Part 2,
1914-74* (1977), ch. 18.

## Chapter X (The Land)

*V.C.H. Staffs.*, vi, articles on agriculture to 1975: 'Pleas of the Forest, Stafford-
shire', ed. G. Wrottesley, *S.H.C.*, v (1); 'Alrewas Court Rolls, 1259-1262', ed.
W. N. Landor, *S.H.C.*, new ser. x (1); 'Alrewas Court Rolls, 1268-1269 and
1272-1273', ed. W. N. Landor, *S.H.C.*, 1910; H. B. Thomas, 'The Enclosure of
Open Fields and Commons in Staffordshire', *S.H.C.*, 1931; W. E. Tate, 'A
Handlist of English Enclosure Acts and Awards. Staffordshire', *S.H.C.*,
1941; R. A. Pelham, 'The 1801 Crop Returns for Staffordshire in their
Geographical Setting', *S.H.C.*, 1950 and 1951; 'Court Rolls of the Manor
of Tunstall', *T.N.S.F.C.*, lix-lxxvi; R. A. Hilton, 'Lord and Peasant in Staffordshire in the Middle Ages', *N.S.J.F.S.*, x, reprinted in R. H. Hilton, *The
English Peasantry in the Later Middle Ages* (1975); Sir Reginald Hardy,

*Court Rolls of the Parish of Tatenhill* (1898); J. E. C. Peters, *The Development of Farm Buildings in Western Lowland Staffordshire up to 1800* (1969).

### Chapter XI (Potteries and Black Country)

*V.C.H. Staffs.*, ii (1967), articles on various industries: *The Blackcountryman* (Black Country Society, 1968 to date); F. Brook, *The Industrial Archaeology of the British Isles: 1—The West Midlands* (1977); D. Dilworth, *The Tame Mills of Staffordshire* (1976); E. Meteyard, *The Life of Josiah Wedgwood* (2 vols., 1865, 1866); R. Sherlock, *The Industrial Archaeology of Staffordshire* (1976); W. J. Thompson, *Industrial Archaeology of North Staffordshire* (1974).

### Chapter XII (Roads, Canals and Railways)

*V.C.H. Staffs.*, ii, articles on 'Roads', 'Canals', 'Railways'; A. L. Thomas, *Geographical Aspects of the Development of Transport and Communications affecting the Pottery Industry of North Staffordshire during the Eighteenth century* (*S.H.C.*, 1934, pt. 1); R. Christiansen and R. W. Miller, *The North Staffordshire Railway* (1971); C. H. Hadfield, *Canals of the West Midlands* (1969 edn.): J. I. Langford, *A Towpath Guide to the Staffordshire and Worcestershire Canal* (1974); *The Knotty* (1970: script of a musical documentary on the North Staffordshire Railway first presented at the *Victoria* theatre, Stoke on Trent, in 1966; introduction and notes by P. Cheesman); *Staffordshire Roads 1700–1840* (Staffordshire County Council Education Department, Local History Source Book G.1, 1975 edn.).

### Chapter XIII (the Civilised Social Life)

*V.C.H. Staffs.*, vol. vi, article on 'Stafford'; vol. viii, articles on 'Newcastle-under-Lyme' and 'Stoke-on-Trent'; vol. xvii, articles on 'West Bromwich', 'Smethwick', 'Walsall'; N. A. Cope, *Stone in Staffordshire* (1972); J. F. Ede, *History of Wednesbury* (1962); G. P. Mander and N. W. Tildesley, *A History of Wolverhampton* (1960).

# Index

Drayton Bassett, 17–18
Dudley, 15–16, 93, 108; castle, 16, 64–7; priory, 16
Dudley, earl of, *see* Ward
Dunston, 42
Dyott, Anthony, 61; Richard, 73

Eccleshall, 24, 27, 46, 76–7, 86; Bishop's Wood, 19; castle, 65
Ecton, 87
Elford, 33, 81
Eliot, George, *see* Evans
Elizabeth I, 36, 53–54, 69, 86
Ellastone, 17
Ellenhall, 76
Endon, 94
engineering, 89
Engleton, 22
Essex, earls of, *see* Devereux
Ethelfleda, wife of Ethelred the ealdorman of Mercia, 26
Ethelweald, bishop of Lichfield, 24
Etruria, 87–8, 96, 108
Evans, Mary Ann (George Eliot), 17; Robert, 17

Farewell priory, 50–1, 79
Fauld, 14
Fazeley, 17, 19, 107
Feilding, Basil, earl of Denbigh, 65
Fenner, William, 57
Fenton, 52, 88, 90–1, 105
Ferrers, Anne, 38; Henry de, 28–30, 36, 49; John, 70; Sir Thomas, 38; William de, 3rd earl of Derby, 36; William de, 4th earl of Derby, 35; —, earl of Derby, 83
Ferrers, Baron, *see* Devereux
Finchpath, 85
Finney, Samuel, 74
fireclay, 88
Fisherwick, 21
FitzAnsculf, William, 28
Fitzherbert, Basil Francis, Baron Stafford, 35; Francis Edward, Baron Stafford, 35
Flash, 14
Fleetwood family, 52
Fletcher-Boughey family, 71
flint mills, 90
Foley, Richard, 86
Fowler, Brian, 51, 54; William, 55; family, 54–5
Fox, George, 57
Fradley, 96
Freville family, 38

Froghall, 97
Furnivalle family, 37

Gailey, 99
Galton bridge, 97
Garrick, David, 17
Gaunt, John of, duke of Lancaster, 36, 85
Gell, Sir John, 64–6
Gernon, Ranulph de, earl of Chester, 35, 49
Geva, daughter of Hugh d'Avranches, earl of Chester, 49
Giffard, Bonaventure, 55; Charles, 42, 66; Sir John, 42, 53, 80; John, 42; Peter, 42, 64; Thomas (died 1776), 42; Thomas (died 1823), 42; family, 42, 55, 61, 66, 86
glass industry, 61, 86, 108
Gnosall, 27, 46
Gordon-Walker, Patrick, 75
Gower, Sir Thomas, 39; *and see* Leveson-Gower
Granville, Earl, *see* Leveson-Gower
Great Haywood, *see* Haywood
Greatbach, Thomas, 77
Grindon, 18, 58
gypsum, 14; *and see* alabaster

Hacket, John, bishop of Lichfield and Coventry, 46, 58
Hales, 22
Hallahan, Mother Margaret, 52
Hamps, river, 14
Hampton, John, 79
Hanbury, 24, 85
Hanbury, Sir John de, 85
Handsworth, 52, 56, 89
Hanford, 91, 93
Hanley, 13, 17, 52, 102, 105; Bethesda chapel, 59; Hanley Green, 59; parliamentary representation, 74
Harborne, 52
Harcourt, Sir Simon, 51
Harecastle tunnel, 96
Harrison, Richard, 68; Thomas, 68
Harrowby, Baron, *see* Ryder; earl of, *see* Ryder
Hartshill, 91
Hatherton, 62
Hatherton, Baron, *see* Littleton
Hawkesyard priory, 52
Haywood, 77; Great, 96
Headda, bishop of Lichfield, 45
Helgot (Domesday tenant), 32
Henry IV, as duke of Lancaster, 36

115

Henshawe, Dr., 54
Heveningham, Dorothy, 54
hill forts, 19
Himley, 66
Hindus, 60
Hingley, Noah, 89
Hoar Cross, 46
Holditch, 21
Holland, Henry, 40; Robert de, 77
Hollington, 14
Hopton Heath, battle of, 65
Horninglow, 79
Howard, Mary, Viscountess Stafford (née Stafford), 35; William, Viscount Stafford, 35
Hulton abbey, 85
Hwicce (mixed British and Anglo-Saxon people), 23

Ilam, 18, 27
industries, see alabaster, boots and shoes, brewing, bricks and tiles, cloth, coal, copper, cotton, engineering, glass, iron, nailmaking, pottery, quarrying, salt, silk
Ingestre, 46
Ingram, Hugo Meynell Francis, 46
Ipstones, 58, 81
iron industry, 14–16, 41, 85–9, 97

Jackson, John, 67
Jacobites, 41, 58, 72–3, 94
Jerningham, George, Baron Stafford, 35
Jesuits, 52
Jews, 60
Johnson, Dr. Samuel, 17, 72

Keele, 41, 49, 64, 77, 79, 87; University, 41–2
Kenrick family, 107–8
King's·Bromley, 30
Kingswinford, 28, 97
Kinnersley, Walter, 62
Kinver, 24, 28, 30, 77, 79, 96; Edge, 13, 19; the Hyde, 86; Iverley common, 81
Kinver forest, 30, 32, 81
Kipling, Alice (née MacDonald), 17; John Lockwood, 17; Rudyard, 17
Knypersley, 64

Ladderedge, 14
Laistre, Louis Martin de, 56
Lancaster, duchy of, 30, 36–7; dukes of, see Gaunt, Henry IV

Lancaster, Thomas of, earl of Lancaster, 36, 47; earls of, 30
Lane, Jane, 67; family, 61, 68
Langton, Walter, bishop of Coventry and Lichfield, 45
Lapley, 65, 67; priory, 49, 50
Lawley, Sir Francis, 84
Lee, John, 108
Lee, Rowland, bishop of Coventry and Lichfield, 51, 53
Leek, 14, 17–18, 28, 65, 90, 94, 101, 104
Legge, William, earl of Dartmouth, 59
Leigh, Edward, 61
Leofwine, bishop of Lichfield, 28–9
Letocetum, see Wall
Leveson, Frances, 39; Admiral Sir Richard, 39; Sir Richard, 67; family, 39
Leveson-Gower, Elizabeth, countess of Sutherland, 39; Granville, Earl Granville, 88; John, Earl Gower, 72; William (died 1691), 71; William (died 1756), 72–3; family, 39, 71; and see Sutherland-Leveson-Gower
Lichfield, 14–15, 17, 19, 23–4, 53, 57, 76, 104–5; archbishopric, 24; cathedral, 27, 39, 45–6, 51; during the Civil War, 62, 64, 66; communications, 91, 94, 101; friary, 50; parliamentary representation, 61, 69–74
Lichfield (also Chester, Coventry, Coventry and Lichfield, Lichfield and Coventry), bishops of, 40, 42, 45–6; and see Baynes, Bentham, Chad, Clinton, Ethelweald, Hacket, Headda, Lee, Leofwine, Limesey, Meuland, Peche, Peter, Sampson, Stavensby
Lichfield, earls of, Viscount, see Anson
Limesey, Robert de, bishop of Chester, 45–6
limestone, 14, 88
Littleton, Edward Richard, Baron Hatherton, 83; family, 86
Loch, James, 83
Long Low, 18
Longbirch, 55
Longford, Sir Ralph, 51
Longton, 52, 88
Lower Elkstone, 81
Loxley, 62

MacDonald, Alexander, 74; Alice, *see* Kipling; Georgiana, *see* Burne-Jones; Louisa, *see* Baldwin
Maer, 19
Manifold, river, 14, 18
Marchington, 19, 26, 81
Marmion, Robert de, 37
Marnham family, 43
Marston, 77–8
Mary Queen of Scots, 36–7, 54, 64, 86
Matthews, Sir Stanley, 17
Mavesyn Ridware, 62
Mayfield, 77
Meaford, 93
Meece brook, 16
Mercia, 23–4, 26, 45; earls of, 28, 49; kings of, *see* Offa, Wulfhere
Meuland, Roger, bishop of Coventry and Lichfield, 30, 47
Michael, Grand Duke, 41
Moddershall, 90
Modwen, St, 26
Monetville, 29
Montgomery, Roger of, earl of Shrewsbury, 28
Moorlands, the, 14, 58, 62, 77
Morfael (Celtic leader), 24
Moseley, 56, 67
Mosley, Sir Oswald, 74
Mow Cop, 59
Mucklestone, 18, 56

nailmaking, 86–7, 89
Napley Heath, 56
Needwood forest, 30, 76, 81
Netherton, 89, 97
Newcastle under Lyme, 14, 40–1, 87, 102, 104; castle, 101; communications, 91, 94, 99; parliamentary representation, 67, 69–71, 73–4; Protestant nonconformity, 58–9
Newcomen, Thomas, 89
Newman, Cardinal John Henry, 52, 56
Northampton, earls of, *see* Compton

Offa, king of Mercia, 24, 26
Offlow hundred, 27
Osborne, George, 107
Ossum's Cave, 18

Paget, Henry, earl of Uxbridge, 41; Henry, 1st marquess of Anglesey, 41; Henry, 6th marquess of Anglesey, 41; John, 40; Thomas, Baron

Paget—*cont.*
Paget, 40; William, 1st Baron Paget, 40, 86; William, 4th Baron Paget, 40–1; William, 5th Baron Paget, 41, 61–2; family, 40
Paine, James, 42
Pankhurst, Christabel, 74
Pattingham, 19, 79
Peada, sub-king of the Middle Angles, 24
Peche, Richard, bishop of Coventry, 46, 50
Pecsaetan (Anglian people), 23
Peel, Sir Robert, 1st Bt., 38, 72, 84, 107; Sir Robert, 2nd Bt., 17, 72
Penderel family, 66, 68
Penk, river, 30
Penkhull, 24
Penkridge, 27–8, 46, 86, 99
Penn, 24
Pennocrucium, 19, 21–2
Peter, bishop of Lichfield, 28
Peter of Blois, 47
Pinson, William, 57
Pirehill hundred, 27
poor relief, 70–1, 105
population, 16, 32–3, 59, 76, 79, 102, 104
Potteries, 13–14, 17, 24, 32, 40, 102, 107–8; Chartism, 74; coalfield, 13; communications, 94, 96–7
pottery industry, 13–14, 21, 85, 87–8, 90, 104
Protestant nonconformity, 41, 57–60
Pugin, A. W. N., 37, 57

quarrying, 14, 85–8, 97

Radford bridge, 30
Radmore, 30, 49; abbey, 49, 50
railways, 97–9
Ramshorn, 23
Ranton priory, 51, 76–7
religious houses, 24, 26–7, 36, 39–41, 47–52, 54, 76–9
Ridgway, Job, 59; family, 59
rivers, 15, 93, 96; *and see* Blithe, Churnet, Dane, Dove, Hamps, Manifold, Penk, Sow, Stour, Tame, Tean, Trent
Roaches, the, 14
roads, 21, 91, 93–4, 99, 100
Robert, son of Noel, 76
Rocester, 17, 21, 107; abbey, 77
Roman Catholicism, 42, 51–7, 60
royal free chapels, 46–7, 51

117

Tamsaetan (Anglian people), 23
Tamworth, 15, 17, 26-7, 33, 37, 46, 72, 97, 101; castle, 37-8, 64-5; church, 27, 46; parliamentary representation, 69, 70, 72; Tamworth pig, 84
Tean, river, 90
Teddesley, 83
Tettenhall, 26-7, 46, 94, 105
Thorpe Constantine, 26
Thor's Cave, 18; Fissure, 18
Thorswood House Farm, 18
Thynne, Thomas, Viscount Weymouth, 72
Tipton, 59, 89, 96-7
Tittensor, 91
Tixall, 68
Toeni, Ralph de, 34; Roger de, 29
Totmonslow hundred, 27
Townshend, George, Marquess Townshend, 38, 72; John, Marquess Townshend, 38
trade unionism, 104
Trent, river, 13, 15, 23-4, 26, 30, 33, 40, 47, 90-1, 93, 96; valley, 13, 21, 26, 76, 91
Trent Vale, 21, 85
Trentham, 91; church, 40, 51; Hall, 40, 71, 73; Park, 40; priory, 39, 49, 77
Tunstall, 13, 74, 81, 85, 104-5, 108
Turner's Hill, 16
Tutbury, 29, 33, 66, 85, 101; castle, 29, 36-7, 64, 66; priory, 36, 49, 50, 77

Upper Hulme, 26
Uttoxeter, 17, 28, 35, 38, 64, 66, 77, 82, 87, 94
Uxbridge, earl of, see Paget

Verdun, Bertram de, 37, 51; family, 37
Vernon family, 37

Wall (formerly Letocetum), 19, 21, 24
Walsall, 24, 30, 56-7, 60-2, 77, 86-7, 89, 94, 99, 101-2, 104-5; industries, 86-7, 89; parliamentary representation, 73
Walton, as place-name, 24
Walton, Izaak, 16-17
Ward, William, earl of Dudley, 73

Warslow, 81
Waterhouses, 23
Watling Street, 19, 21, 23, 26, 93-4, 99
Watt, James, 89
Wedgwood, Josiah, 17, 87-8, 94, 96, 107-8
Wednesbury, 24, 58, 73, 89, 93-4
Wednesfield, 24
Weeford, 93
Werburgh, St, 24
Wesley, John, 58-9, 102
West Bromwich, 17, 44, 50, 60, 89, 94, 97, 100, 102, 105, 107-8; Manor House, 43; parliamentary representation, 74
West Indians, 60
West Midlands, county of, 16
Weston under Lizard, 19
Wetton, 18
Weymouth, Viscount, see Thynne
Whieldon, Thomas, 88
Whiteladies House (Salop.), 66
Whitgreave, Thomas (living 1651), 67; Thomas (living 1780), 56
Whitmore, 99
Whorwood, John, 81
Wightman, Edward, 57
Wilkinson, John, 88-9
Willenhall, 90
William I, 28-30, 32, 36, 42, 47
Wint, Peter de, 17
Witham, Dr. George, 55
Wolseley bridge, 91
Wolseley, Erasmus, 54
Wolverhampton, 30, 39, 104-5; church, 27, 46-7, 51; during the Civil War, 64, 66; communications, 94, 96-7, 100; industries, 87; parliamentary representation, 73-4; population, 102; Protestant nonconformity, 57; Roman Catholicism, 55-7
wool trade, 77
Wootton under Weaver, 14
Wrottesley, Sir Richard, 72
Wulfhere, king of Mercia, 24
Wyatt, James, 46; Samuel, 42
Wychnor, 23, 91
Wulfric Spot, 27, 47

Yoxall, 77